WILLIAM MORRIS

Redesigning the World

John Burdick

TODTRI

This book was designed and produced by
Todtri Productions Limited
P.O. Box 572, New York, NY 10116-0572
FAX: (212) 279-1241

Printed and bound in Singapore

ISBN 0-7651-9249-7

Author: John Burdick

Publisher: Robert M. Tod
Editorial Director: Elizabeth Loonan
Book Designer: Mark Weinberg
Senior Editor: Cynthia Sternau
Project Editor: Ann Kirby
Photo Editor: Laura Wyss
Production Coordinator: Jay Weiser
Desktop Associate: Paul Kachur
Typesetting: Command-O Design

Picture Credits

Art Resource, New York 21

Michael Boys/© Corbis 27, 54

Bridgeman/Art Resource 14, 47, 77

Corbis-Bettmann 37, 96, 97, 102, 109, 111, 113, 123

Hulton Getty , London 7 (bottom), 15 (top), 15 (bottom), 17, 18, 20,
34, 42, 45, 46, 58, 59, 82, 92, 94, 101, 103, 107, 117, 122

Lauros-Giraudon/Art Resource 26

Erich Lessing/Art Resource 31

Pierpont Morgan Library, New York/Art Resource 23, 98

Tate Gallery, London/Art Resource 16, 28, 32, 34, 38, 39, 40–41

UPI/Corbis-Bettmann 44, 108

Victoria & Albert Museum, London/Art Resource 5, 6, 22, 24–25, 30, 31, 47,
50, 51, 60, 64, 66, 67, 68–69, 70, 71, 72–73, 76, 77, 78, 80, 83, 84–85,
87, 88–89, 91, 95, 110, 119, 120, 124, 127

Victoria & Albert Museum, London/Superstock 8–9, 10, 13, 19, 29, 48, 52–53, 55,
56–57, 62–63, 74, 79, 86, 90, 115, 118, 125

William Morris Gallery, London 7 (top), 12, 36, 49, 69 (top),
75, 81, 99, 100, 104, 106, 112, 114, 126

A

CONTENTS

INTRODUCTION

*A*brief review of the life of William Morris is likely to leave one wondering, "where does all my time go?" As an artist, poet, political writer, activist, and public figure, Morris was astonishingly prolific. His collected writings total twenty-four large volumes, a body of poetry, prose romances, and political essays that alone would constitute a formidable life's work. Of course, Morris was far more than a writer. In fact, his reputation today relies less on his poetry (for which he was best known in his own time) and more on his plentiful and unforgettable textile designs, his revolutionary decorative arts business, and his work as a somewhat unlikely and controversial socialist. Beyond his prodigious output lies the marvel of his mastery and his lasting influence; everything Morris touched, he changed. Any in-depth discussion of modern architecture, poetry, decor, arts and crafts, book printing, or socialism will eventually mention his name, sometimes as a curious aside, sometimes as an indispensable landmark. The modern scholar or general reader, exhausted by following his tracks through the heart of the nineteenth-century, will begin to suspect that days then must have been several hours longer.

If Morris's staggering productivity can be explained at all, it will be by this fairly simple formula. Start with a boy of boundless energy and intelligence in a world without electronic sedatives. Place him in affluent surroundings and insure that money will never be an issue. Isolate him in his youth so that the inventions of his imagination are his chief companions. Shape that imagination with nothing but the best: unspoiled nature, medieval arts and architecture, Arthurian legend. Educate him the expensive way. After his formal schooling, introduce him

to a few charismatic and dynamic mentors—painters, poets, and thinkers who will model the life of the artist and identify him as one of their own. For motivation, situate him in a vital and turbulent era in which opposing forces vie to determine the direction of a culture. For support, surround him with a fraternity of the like-minded, an idealistic brotherhood inspired as much by their contempt for the way things are as by their passion for the way things might be. To prevent complacency, endow him with a sensitive conscience that will not let him rest and will spur him on endlessly to new enterprises and frontiers. Through it all, feed him well. Voila: William Morris.

The main difficulty in understanding Morris lies not in accounting for his fecundity and productivity—some people just do more—but in finding the cohesion, the unifying consistency at the bottom of his diverse endeavors. It would be a disservice not to let Morris explain himself in his own words, especially since he expressed his essence so many times and so variously. "Apart from my desire to produce beautiful things," Morris said in one of his many public lectures, "the leading passion of my life is hatred of modern civilisation." The two passions he mentions are clearly one. Morris was driven like few others to create, and all of his creations shared a common purpose: to oppose what he saw as the bland tedium, greed, and degraded tastes of the Victorian industrial world and to restore the power of art in everyday life.

These driving forces were present from the very beginning of his life. William Morris was born in the English countryside just miles removed from industrial London. The two conflicting kinds of imagery—meadows, flowers,

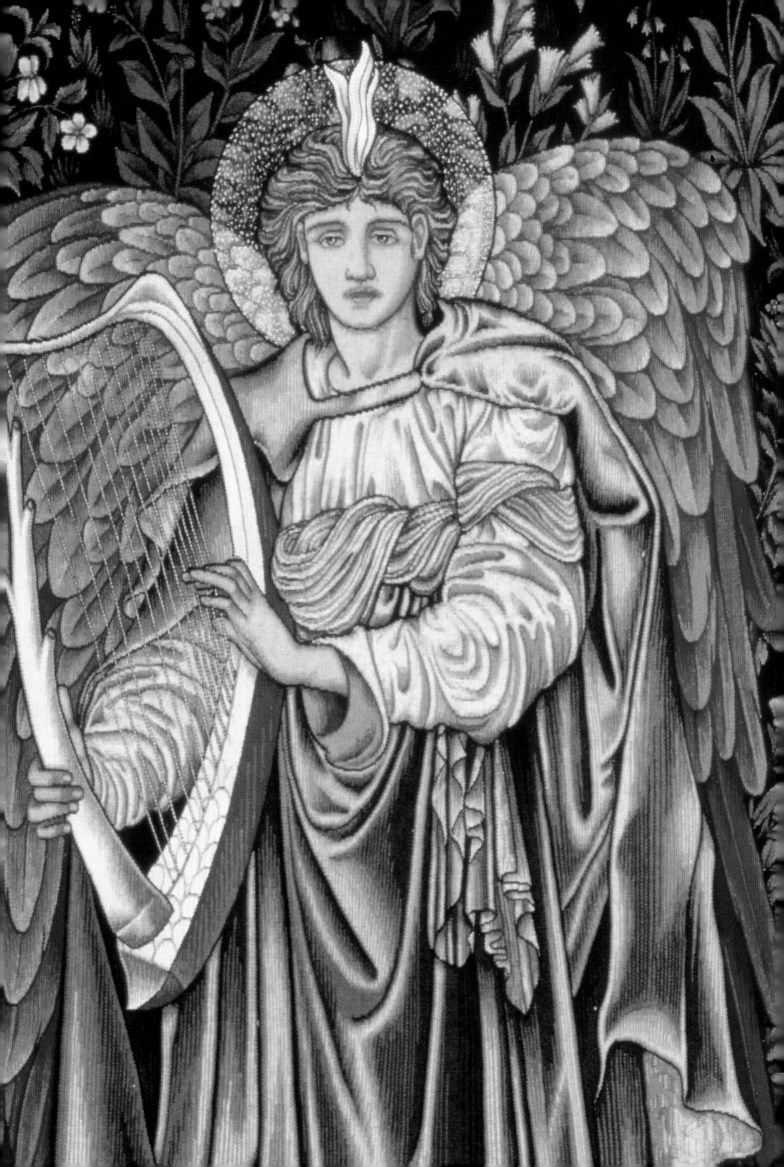

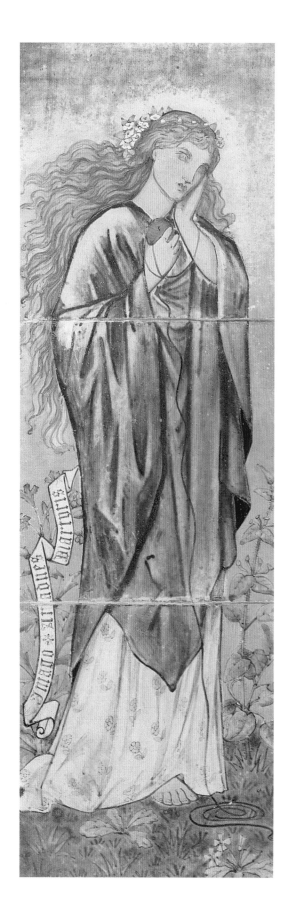

Ariadne

WILLIAM MORRIS, 1870; glazed ceramic tile. Victoria & Albert Museum, London. Due to his diverse talents, William Morris might be called a Renaissance man today, but he would have objected to the label. Morris and his friends blamed the Renaissance period for the separation of design and production in decorative arts.

and birds on one hand and factories, pollution, and urban squalor on the other—combined to form his artistic and social sensibility at a young age. His work expressed a tension, a tenuous balance between dream and reality, the aesthetic and the functional, visions of an idyllic past and of an idealistic future. In the difficult present in which he was forced to live, Morris struggled to find an identity that would embrace and reconcile these schisms.

He wore many hats, assumed many personas, and left a remarkable legacy of influential work. Although he never designed a building himself, he still managed to became a significant influence on modern architecture through his work with prominent architects G.E. Street and Philip Webb, and his founding of Anti-Scrape, a movement dedicated to the preservation of old buildings. He was not a gifted painter, but his friendship and collaborations with Edward Burne-Jones and Dante Gabriel Rossetti afford him a meaningful place in that tradition as well. As a young man, he rejected organized religion, but the stained-glass windows and tapestries produced by Morris & Co. (the firm he started and supported), were key elements in a widespread revival of ecclesiastical arts. He had very little interest or talent in running a business, but Morris & Co. revolutionized interior decor and set the stage for the famous arts and crafts movement in Britain and America. He was, in addition, a beloved poet, a respected translator of Icelandic literature, an influential book printer, and, some contend, an early environmentalist.

Still, he searched for more ways to change the Victorian social conditions that so repelled him. It was his somewhat troubled conscience that led him to his most controversial and puzzling identity as a socialist. In his time, few could understand why a wealthy man of refined tastes would reinvent himself as a shockingly revolutionary socialist, why a passionate admirer of medieval art and culture would dirty his hands with contemporary politics. In his early years, he believed producing (and selling) beautiful things was enough, a satisfactory way of

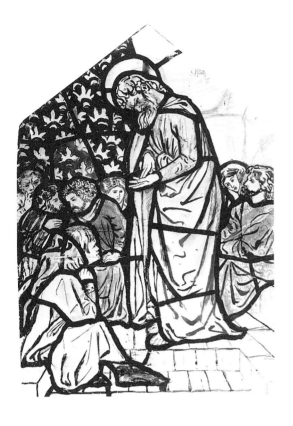

beautifying an ugly world. As he grew older, he began to understand the relationship between social climate and quality of art. Something is amiss in society if the fruits of culture, namely the creation and appreciation of fine art, are not within the grasp of all citizens, as, in his era, they certainly were not.

When his effort to infuse common life with uncommon beauty succeeded only in altering the tastes of the already wealthy and cultured, Morris adopted a more radical approach and took his mission to the streets. He began to believe that healthy art was not possible in an ill society. In this transformation, there is the unmistakable flavor of compensation and guilt. Morris would never be fully comfortable with his wealth, but he was less comfortable with the idea of giving it up. His life and work would be fraught with contradictions and vulnerable to well-founded charges of hypocrisy. Far from letting them paralyze him, however, Morris seemed to draw power from such paradoxes.

All issues of consistency and contradiction aside, it is a joy to get to know this remarkable man through his works, the anecdotes of his close friends and associates, and the observations of the many prominent and famous people he encountered and influenced. Big, hearty, temperamental, and endearing, Morris impressed those who met him with his energy, his passion for art, his generosity, and his authenticity. By all reports, he could not for the life of him stop talking, yet people were thrilled to witness his broad intelligence and intoxicating imagination in action. Similarly, he could not stop working. He loved nothing more than a day spent absorbed in the process of creation. He relished the minutia, in his own words, the "drudgery" of all the arts. He was an exemplary craftsman, providing a model of versatility and focus for the many who worked with him. For a renowned artist and poet, he was refreshingly unaffected. He was a faithful friend, a loving father, and, despite the marital trouble that was the chief source of anguish in his life, a caring husband. He died at the relatively young age of sixty-two from what appeared to be total exhaustion. No man of his generation, or perhaps of any other, worked so hard and tried so exuberantly and productively to redesign the world in the image of beauty and brotherhood.

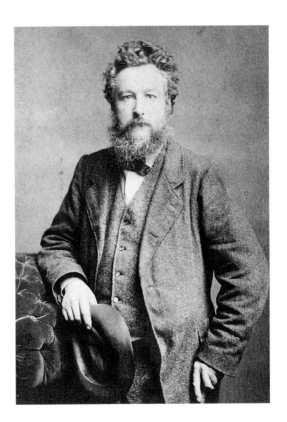

St. Paul Preaching at Athens

WILLIAM MORRIS, c. 1860s; cartoon for stained-glass window. William Morris Gallery, London. St. Paul Preaching at Athens would eventually appear in Selsley Church, Gloucestershire. It was one of Morris's more than 100 stained-glass designs.

William Morris

1875; archival photograph. The Hulton Getty Picture Collection Limited. Those familiar with Morris's art and poetry were often surprised to discover how disheveled and unassuming he was in person.

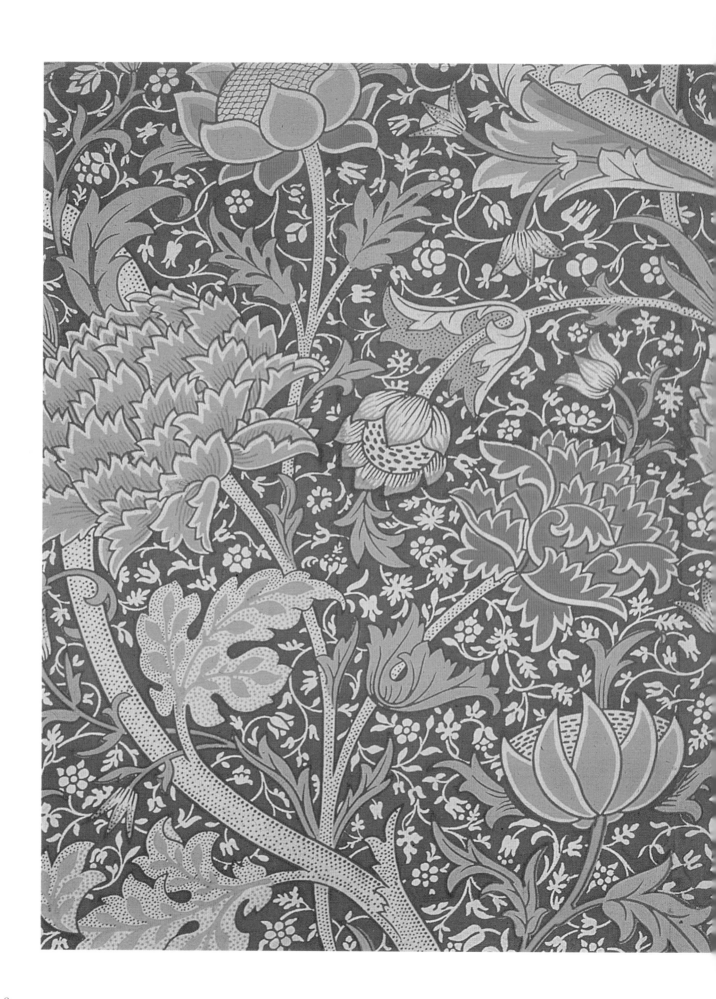

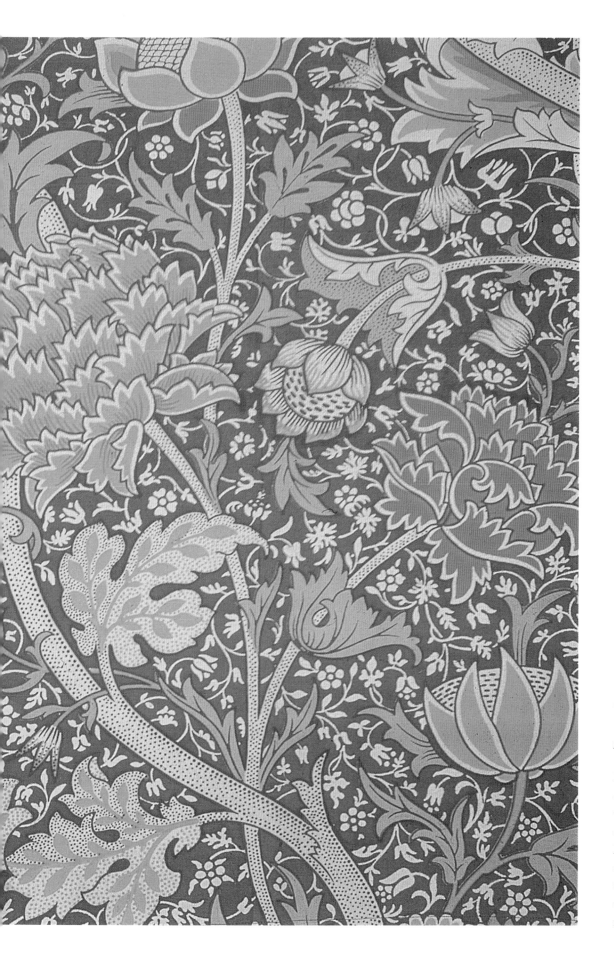

Cray

*WILLIAM MORRIS, 1884;
printed cotton. Victoria
& Albert Museum, London.*
Printed at Morris's
own Merton Abbey
works, *Cray* is gener-
ally considered to be
Morris's most intricate
and expensive design.
Of all his printed cot-
tons, it required the
most printing blocks.

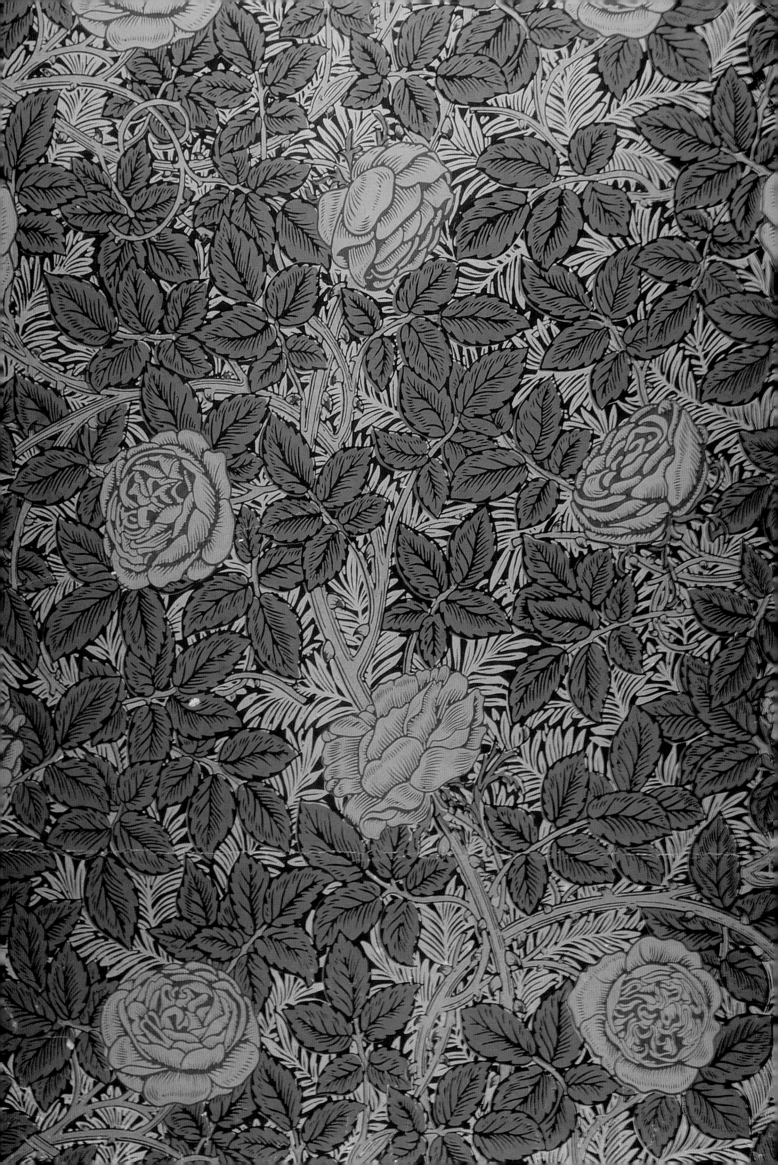

Chapter One

BEGINNINGS: THE EARLY LIFE AND EDUCATION OF WILLIAM MORRIS

As he himself readily admitted, William Morris might never have become a poet, master designer, and prominent socialist had he not been born into an affluent family in an idyllic community. The great champion of fine art for all people understood that "anyone who professes to think that the question of art and cultivation must go before that of the knife and fork . . . does not understand what art means, or how that its roots must have a soil of a thriving and unanxious life." The mortal enemies of Morris the socialist—capitalism, industrialism, and the Victorian social hierarchy—were the very forces that afforded him the leisure to follow his creative impulses, to dwell in a world of imagination and learning untroubled by the impositions of the knife and fork.

To his credit, Morris neither denied this contradiction nor disavowed his advantaged upbringing. Instead, he set his boundless energy and troubled conscience to work for an idealistic and classless society, a tricky and perilous enterprise for a privileged individual. In many ways the world Morris left bore less resemblance to his ideal world than the one he entered. But in the startlingly diverse forms in which Morris expressed himself—his famous wallpapers, stained-glass, tapestries, furniture,

poetry, and essays and lectures—he left behind if not the blueprints for then the still alluring spirit of a society united by an appreciation of art and meaningful labor; a world in which, "the perception and creation of beauty, the enjoyment of real pleasure that is, shall be felt to be as necessary to man as his daily bread."

The third of nine children, and the eldest son, William Morris was born on March 24, 1834, at Elm House in Walthamstow, a rural community outside London. His father, also William Morris, was a London bill broker who had moved his family out of the city the year before William was born. When a small investment in the Devonshire copper mines paid huge dividends in 1840, the Morrises moved to Woodford Hall, a Palladian mansion on fifty acres surrounded by Epping Forest. Thus, with the wealth gained from the burgeoning industrialization of England, a historical development that would later offend William Morris's aesthetic and political sensibilities to no end, young William was delivered to a romantic playground devoid of urban filth and industrial eyesores, a pristine landscape that would inspire his poetry and his designs throughout his life.

In addition to being a successful capitalist, William senior was also a deeply religious

Lea Wallpaper

WILLIAM MORRIS, n.d.; print design. Victoria & Albert Museum, London. Of all the designs and products created by Morris & Co., Morris's wallpapers are the only ones still commercially available today, a true testament to their popular appeal.

Woodford Hall, Essex

Drawing; William Morris Gallery, London. In 1839, Morris's middle-class father purchased 272 shares of the Devonshire copper mines at the cost of one pound per share. Within a year, their value had risen to £800 each. The newly wealthy Morrises moved to this palladian mansion in Essex, and young William's financial future was secure.

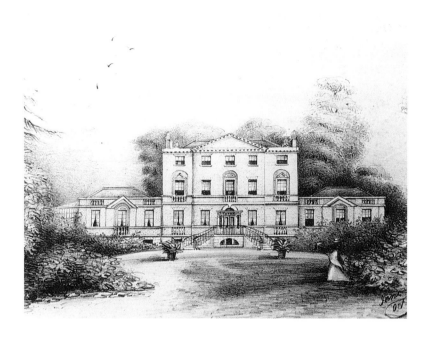

Rose Design

WILLIAM MORRIS, c. 1880s. Victoria & Albert Museum, London. Morris's childhood in Epping Forest no doubt influenced his designs. The colors, brambles, and birds of the forest became recurrent themes in his wallpapers, tapestries, and carpets.

evangelical Protestant, and that may explain how the Morrises avoided some of the trappings of great and sudden wealth. An admirer of the Middle Ages, the older Morris insisted on a spare and functional household and a highly ritualized, old fashioned approach to everyday living. His children were introduced early to the disciplines of bread baking and butter churning, rigid meal times, and church duties. William senior, however, does not appear to have been a warm or accessible father. Had he lived to witness William junior's adult life, he surely would have been outraged by his son's repudiation of capitalism (in theory) and of religion, a break from the familial tradition paid for, no less, by the son's considerable annual salary from the family estate. Yet, in many ways the Morris household did provide William with the "soil of a thriving and unanxious life," and not merely in terms of wealth and security.

In *News From Nowhere*, the Utopian romance that Morris published late in life, the ideal socialist future bears a telling resemblance to the England of Morris's childhood, or at least to the rural environs of Epping Forest. In Morris's twenty-first century, factories have all but disappeared from the landscape; some do exist, but only enough to release people from the most tedious labor, not to enslave them to it. The only place money can be found is in museums. Wildlife flourishes, and all man-made structures evince the highest craft, functionality, and beauty—reflections of the joy the builders took in creating them. Similarly, Morris's childhood paradise was unblemished, although financed, by factories and exploitation; money was so abundant as to seem unimportant. What has changed, in *News From Nowhere*, is the basis of society and the class divide, the ugly dichotomies of rich and poor, privileged and forgotten. As if to expiate his guilt, in Morris' Utopia, all children are as free and fortunate as he was.

Epping Forest and Marlborough: The School of Nature

As a sickly boy (who became a most robust adult), Morris took long walks in the country-side for his health. It was here that his most meaningful and lasting education began. He observed and learned the curves of flowers, the tangled logic of thickets and brambles, and the colors of birds, all of which would later appear repeatedly in his wallpapers, tapestries, and carpets. William's companions were nature and fantasy more often than siblings or other children. He rode his pony through the forest dressed in his own suit of armor, his imagination fueled by the novels of Sir Walter Scott. As an artist, Morris would excel at illustrations of plants and natural scenes, but, by his own admission and the consensus of history, was not good at representing human forms (and, some attest, not much better at conducting romantic relationships). In this way, his art consistently

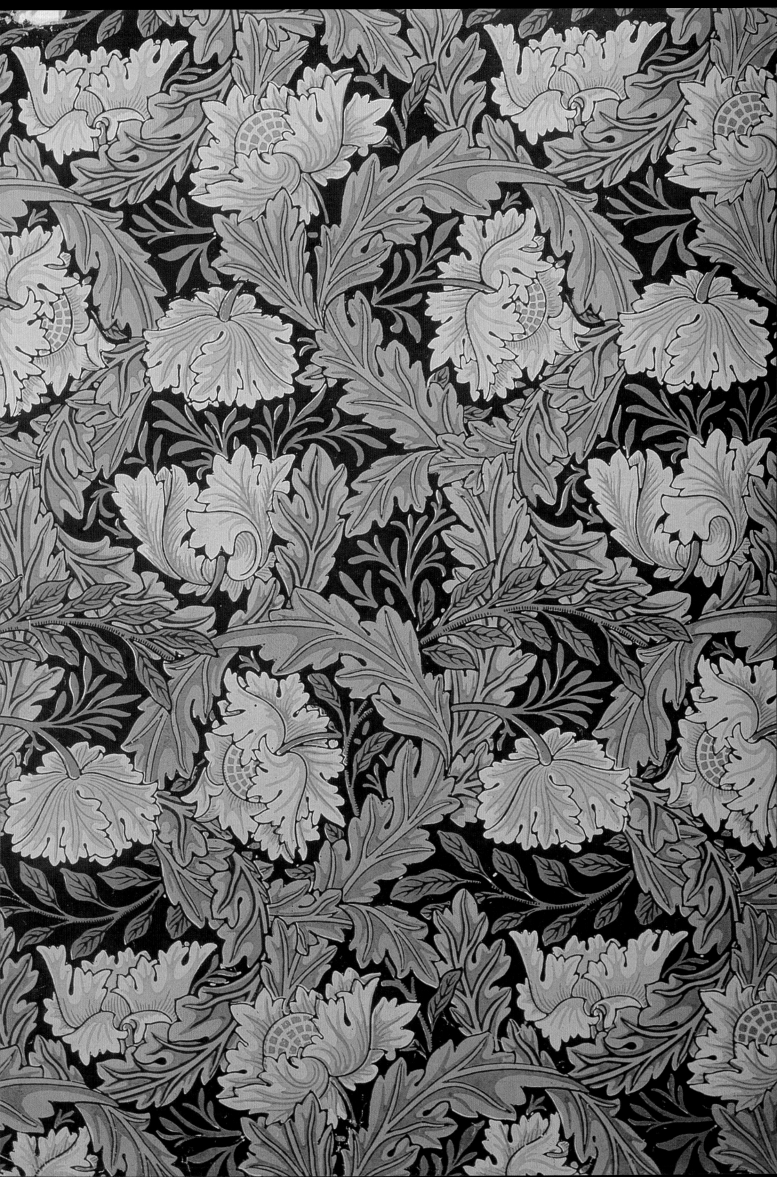

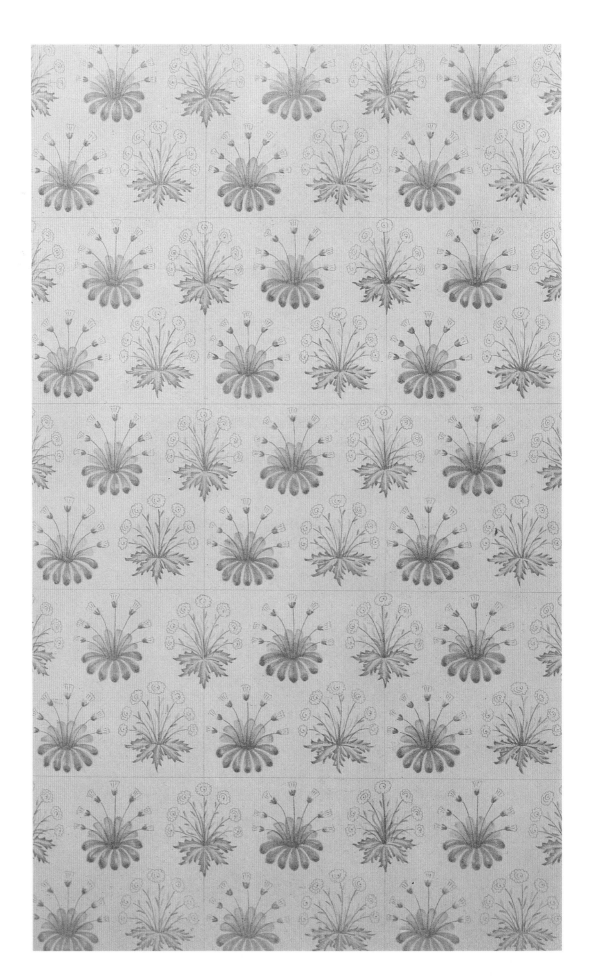

Daisy

WILLIAM MORRIS,
c. 1860s; textile design.
Victoria & Albert
Museum, London.
This pattern shows
up repeatedly in
Morris's early
designs: as an em-
broidery, a chintz,
a wallpaper. Many
designs were used
in several different
media, especially
if they proved
to be popular.

expressed the experience of a solitary and mentally absorbed boy.

Morris's lifelong interest in architecture and interior design, and his decidedly medieval bias, may also have taken shape in the wilds of Epping Forest, itself a kind of medieval preserve. When not indulging in knightly fantasies in the woods, William enjoyed exploring the local Essex churches, making note of their fine brass work. His favorite spot was Queen Elizabeth I's hunting lodge at nearby Chingford Hatch in Epping Forest. One room in particular, a room "hung with faded greenery," would serve as a frequent touchstone when, in later years, Morris would transform the look and feel of Victorian interiors. At eight years of age, Morris visited Canterbury Cathedral with his father. It was his first exposure to a classic specimen of Gothic architecture. Although his own apprenticeship in architecture in the 1850s was short-lived, his enduring fascination with all things medieval and his commitment to the preservation of old buildings may well have their origins in this first revelation of Canterbury.

In 1848, the same year as his father's death, Morris attended Marlborough boarding school in the Wiltshire district. The rest of the family left the grand accommodations of Woodford Hall and moved to Water House, a smaller but still opulent mansion in Walthamstow. At Marlborough, Morris continued his largely unsupervised education. The school had been founded in 1843 primarily to provide a privileged education to the sons of clergymen, and, later, to anyone else who could afford it. But in its early years, Marlborough was grossly over-crowded and poorly organized. Such conditions allowed Morris to dictate his own curriculum—mostly books of architecture and archaeology—and to roam at will through the Wiltshire

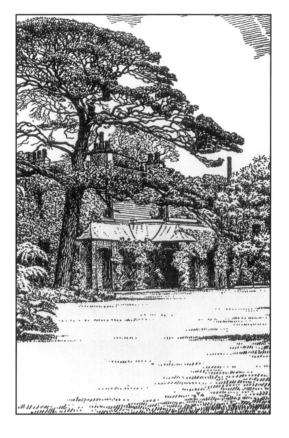

Elm House, Walthamstow

The Hulton Getty Picture Collection limited.
William Morris was born at Elm House and lived there until age six. When his father died in 1848, the Morrises returned to Walthamstow and took up residence in Water House.

countryside, the Savernake Forest, and the stone circles at Averbury. In essence, Morris graduated from one splendid wonderland to another, his fantasy-trances growing ever more particular as he learned more of English landscapes and legends.

It was also at Marlborough that Morris began to discover his force as a public personality, a

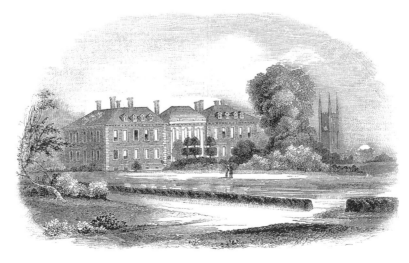

Marlborough Collegiate School

The Hulton Getty Picture Collection Limited.
Disorganization and lax discipline at Marlborough allowed Morris to continue his self-education. His memories of the school were not entirely fond ones, but one of his Marlborough schoolmates read at his funeral almost fifty years later.

15

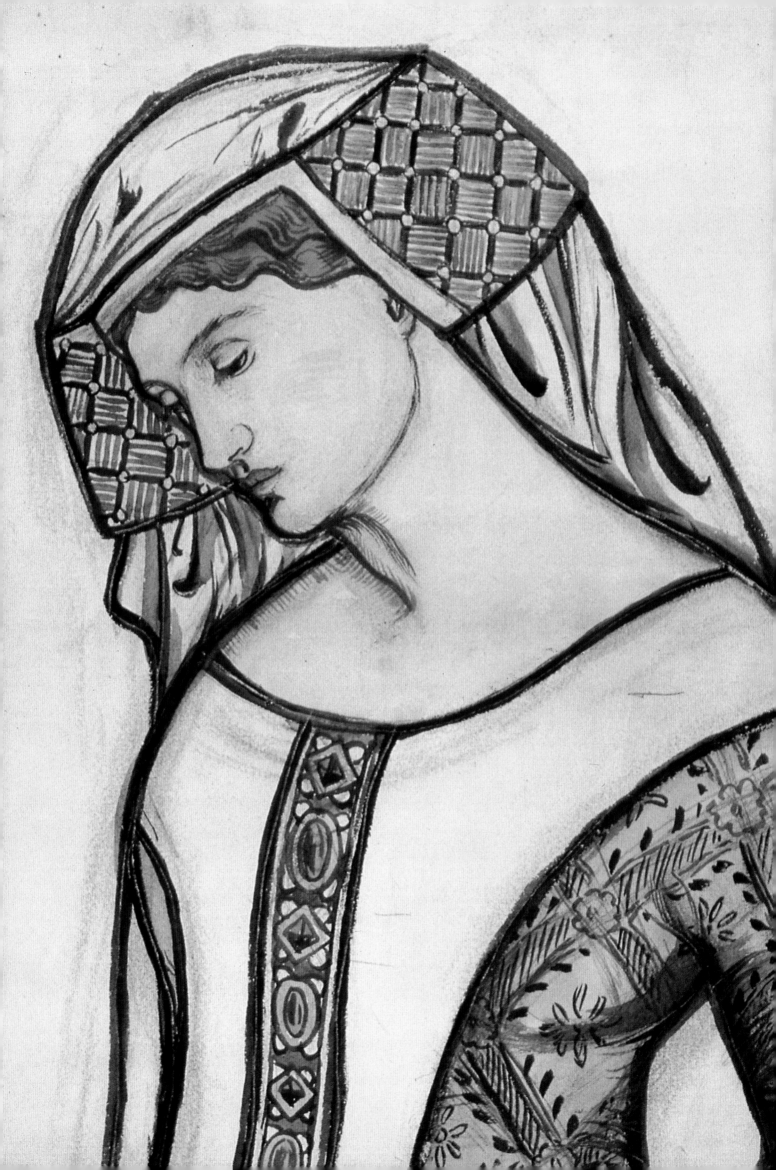

kind of charisma due in part to his large size and heartiness, and in part to his restless mental energy and verbosity. Morris loved to tell stories and recite verses for hours at a time, a practice he would continue throughout his life, whether the audience be Marlborough school chums or such literary figures as George Bernard Shaw and William Butler Yeats. His friendships seem to have been based less on dialogue and mutual exchange than on intoxicating narratives and compelling convictions; Morris would forever hold the center of attention. Perhaps he was unwilling or unable to relinquish it.

Thus was the artist's aesthetic and emotional disposition formed from a sensual appreciation of nature and a myth-inspired, romantic imagination. As is the case with so many artists, the dreamy, self-sufficient child never really left Morris. He was able to summon that child at will, to tune out the distractions of an often repellent adult world and turn himself with singular focus toward the tasks of designing or writing. And, like so many artists, Morris was often perceived as a spoiled child, out of touch with others, communicating solely through self-absorbed monologue. Morris left Marlborough after a student riot in 1851. A year later, he was accepted into Exeter College, Oxford,

probably with the intention of taking Holy Orders and beginning a career in the Church. This was certainly his family's expectation, and Morris too found it an attractive notion. He was moved by the high ritual and beautiful art of Anglicanism, and the recent Oxford Movement, stressing the social responsibility of the Church, appealed to his sense of altruism. But Oxford would provide him with something far more valuable than a career, something conspicuously absent from his childhood: the companionship of kindred spirits.

Oxford at Mid-Century

In his later years, William Morris would tell a young George Bernard Shaw that the money that went into his Oxford education was the only money he felt he had wasted in his life. By this, the sometimes hyperbolic Morris meant to debunk the myth of the cultured Oxford man and the inherited wisdom and power of the privileged classes. But Morris certainly understood that his years at Oxford were some of the most significant and formative in his life; in an emotional letter to his mother written at the end of his Oxford career, he insisted that, "your money has by no means been thrown away." At Oxford, Morris found himself at the heart of

Oxford

Late nineteenth century; archival photograph. The Hulton Getty Picture Collection Limited.
As a young man, Morris was immediately taken by Oxford's medieval character. He maintained ties with the university throughout his life, returning as a famous man in the 1880s and shocking the faculty with a speech on the necessity of a socialist revolution.

Guinevere

detail; WILLIAM MORRIS, 1858; oil on canvas; 28¼ x 19¾ in. (71.7 x 50.1 cm). The Tate Gallery, London.
Morris and his Pre-Raphaelite brothers created a wealth of work inspired by Arthurian legends. Morris was not well regarded as a painter, but the heavy lines of his *Guinevere* are in many ways similar to those of stained-glass, a medium Morris mastered.

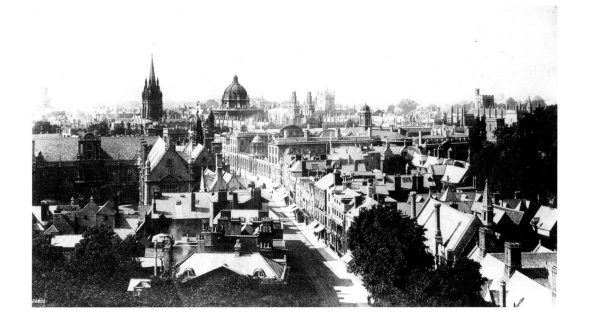

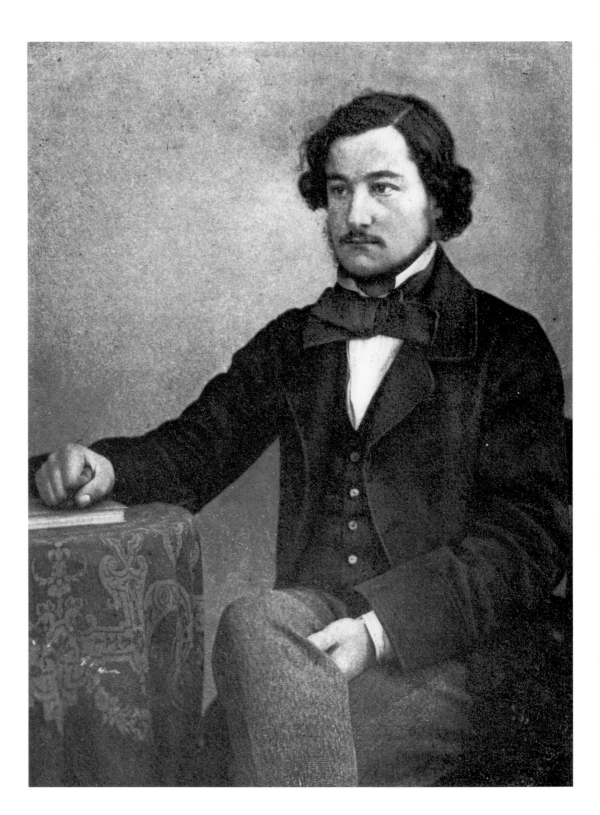

William Morris

*1857; archival photograph.
The Hulton Getty Picture
Collection Limited.*
Taken at the close of
his Oxford years, this
photograph portrays
Morris at a time when
he was deciding be-
tween a Church career
and a life spent de-
voted to art. Around
this time, he re-
nounced his intentions
of taking Holy Orders
and began his appren-
ticeship in the office of
architect G. E. Street.

the tensions and conflicts that defined the age. He discovered a sense of mission, formed his alliances, and recognized his enemies. In all, his years there were a period of personal and social awakening, though not exactly of the kind that Oxford intended.

The Oxford Movement, an effort by prominent clergymen to galvanize Christians and restore the power of the Church in English affairs, had come to an official end in 1845 with John Henry Newman's conversion to Catholicism. However, when Morris arrived at Oxford in 1853, the spirit and resonance of the Tractarians, as the leaders of the Oxford Movement were known, were still very much in the air. At the root of the Tractarian movement was a preference for medieval theocracy and social order over secular government and, in their opinion, its consequent moral decay. It was a preference that extended to art and architecture as well. Rapid industrial growth had taken its toll on old England. As much an aesthetic response to the present as a moral and social one, the Oxford Movement crystallized the widespread sentiment that things were better in the old days, that England, starting with its most prestigious university and intellectual center, would do best not to reform but to regress.

And the Oxford that Morris first encountered did appear to be an intoxicating medieval remnant with its myriad spires and ringing bells. In truth, the modern world was rapidly encroaching, symbolized by the opening of an Oxford railway line, and the medieval splendor was something of a facade, in part the product of a restoration craze that Morris would grow to detest. The piety of its students, too, was perfunctory, imposed from above, and only a minor impediment to the typical collegiate mischief and partying. Even so, the boy whose imagination had taken shape

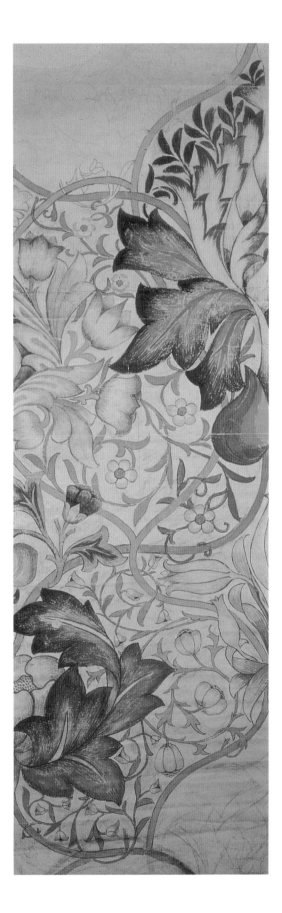

Artichoke

WILLIAM MORRIS, c. 1877; embroidery pattern. Victoria & Albert Museum, London. Artichoke was probably Morris's most popular embroidery design. It was commissioned by Ada Phoebe Goodman for her Philip Webb-designed home.

William Morris and Edward Burne-Jones

1890s, archival photograph. The Hulton Getty Picture Collection Limited. Even when Morris's fervent political activism strained their relationship, Morris continued to dine with the Burne-Jones's every Sunday. After Morris's death in 1896, Burne-Jones said that he felt he had little left to live for.

View of nave with the great organ.

Cathedral, Chartres. Morris and the brotherhood admired not only the art and architecture of medieval Europe; they were equally inspired by the period's social systems and the role of the craftsman as described in Ruskin's *The Stones of Venice.*

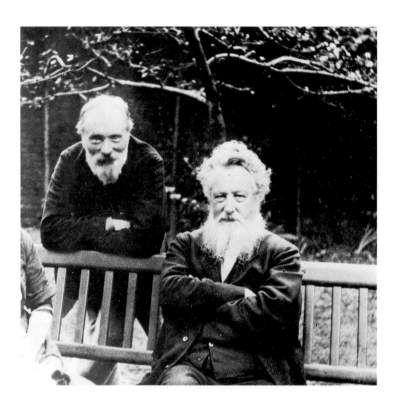

in Epping Forest was easily entranced by the illusion of an old Oxford untouched by the crass hand of progress. Although Morris had never particularly taken to his family's religious convictions, he still responded deeply to the notion of a pious life in the service of goodness, echoes of his knightly fantasies. With that predisposition in a sympathetic environment, Morris seemed destined for a career in the Church. This most likely would have been the case had Morris not found himself the informal leader of a group of his peers, an independent, intellectual community that formed its principles and set out to change the world from a dormitory room at Oxford.

Burne-Jones and the Brotherhood

Edward Burne-Jones, then simply Ted Jones, was the son of a picture framer in Birmingham, and representative of a new kind of Oxford student. Despite a hefty class divide between them, Morris and Burne-Jones became fast friends. Their friendship might well have marked the genesis of Morris's painful awareness of class distinctions and his ultimate commitment to

abolish them. Ironically, the only event that would ever strain their relationship would be Morris's conversion to socialism years after both were already successful artists. At Oxford, the vociferous Morris found companionship and inspiration in the quietly determined Burne-Jones. The solitary rambler of the countryside now had a like-minded partner.

Soon, Burne-Jones introduced Morris to other Birmingham lads, many of whom would become his lifelong friends and associates: Richard Dixon, Charles Faulkner, William Fulford, and others. The group began congregating in Faulkner's rooms in Pembroke College and talking late into the night. In the beginning, they discussed exactly what the Oxford dons would have them discuss: theological and ecclesiastical issues, and the function of the Church in society. Morris himself, as Dixon recalled, played the part of the high-minded and aristocratic Anglican, a persona that no doubt caused him some embarrassment in later years. The group shared a distaste for contemporary social conditions and a borderline fanatical devotion to the art and culture of England in the Middle Ages as they understood it. Their college years coincided with the first great wave of research and scholarship on medieval times, so, as much as they fancied themselves to be renegades, their passions were very much a product of their environment.

Gradually, the group's areas of interest expanded into secular areas, first to poetry, especially Tennyson's adaptations of Malory's Arthurian legends, then to the more difficult works of social theorists such as Thomas Carlyle and John Ruskin, both preeminent intellectuals with medieval longings. Ruskin in

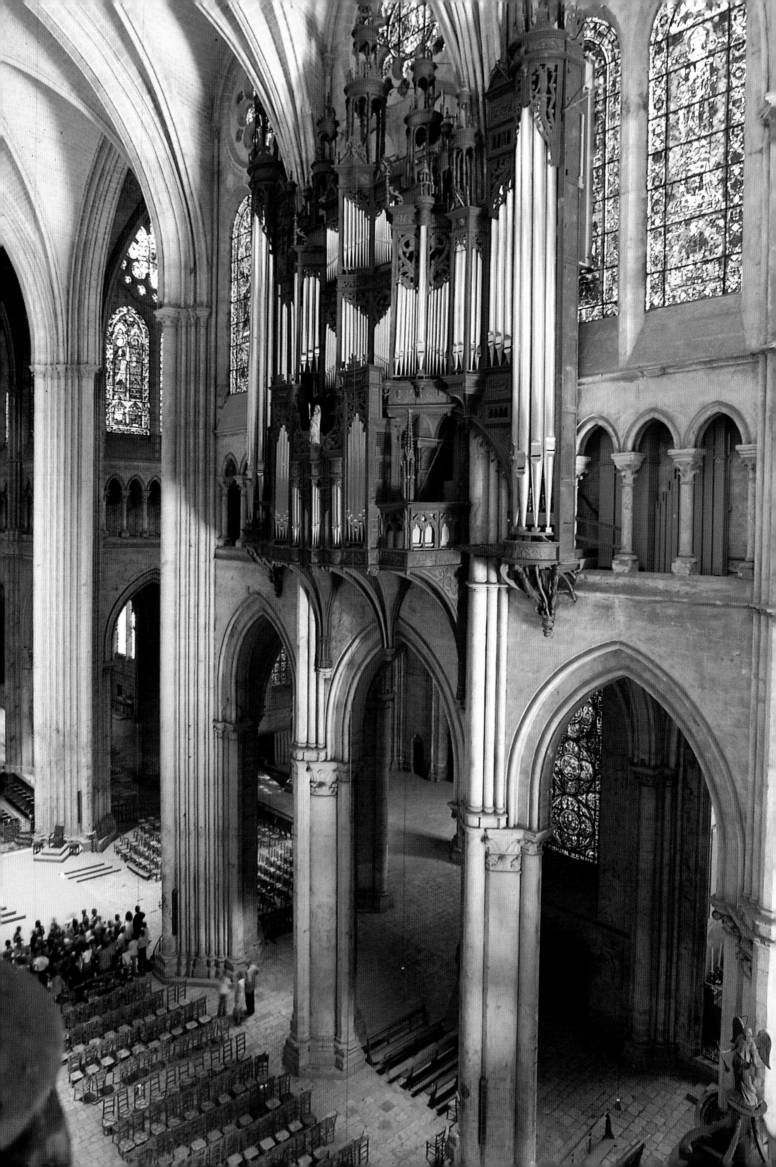

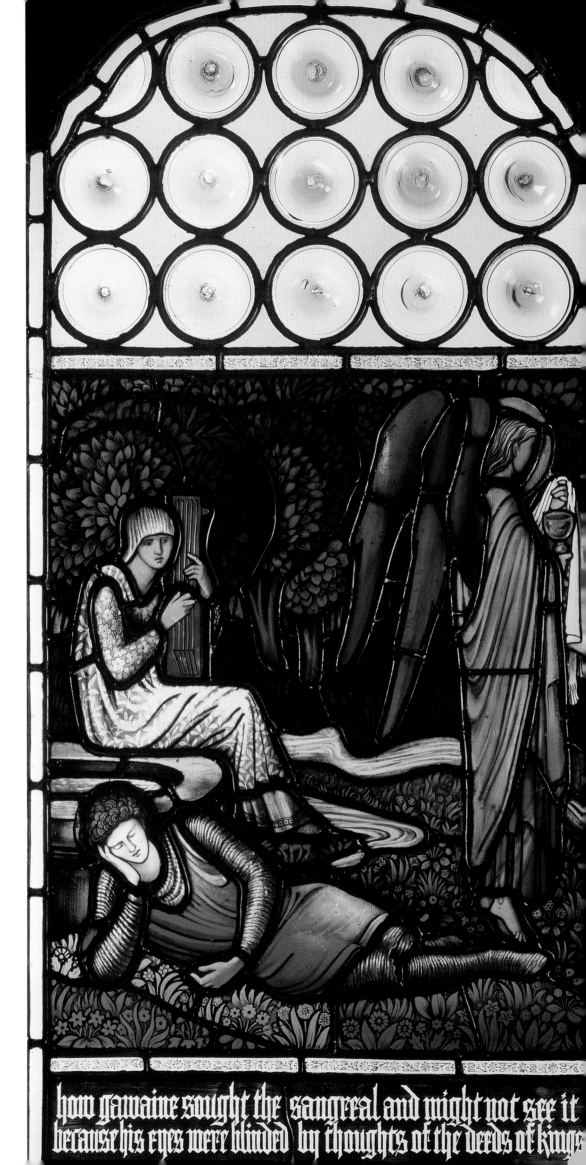

How Gawaine sought the Sang Real and might not see it because his eyes were blinded by thoughts of the deeds of kings

EDWARD BURNE-JONES, executed by William Morris, c. 1880; stained-glass. Victoria & Albert Museum, London. Burne-Jones was by far the most prolific of the firm's stained-glass designers and thought to be the most talented. Burne-Jones's designs were just as often based on English legends of the Middle Ages as on religious stories.

how gawaine sought the sangreal and might not see it
because his eyes were blinded by thoughts of the deeds of kings

particular influenced Morris and his friends. His *The Stones of Venice*, published in 1853, questioned the inherent goodness of progress and suggested that the Middle Ages attained a superior balance of the individual and the community. Ruskin praised the virtues of the communal craftsmen's guilds and argued that the joy taken in labor was indispensable to a healthy civilization. Following Ruskin, Morris grew to hate the specialization of labor characteristic of the industrial era. The Medieval craftsman participated in all aspects of building—stonemasonry, wood carving, etc.—and thus enjoyed a wholesome gratification in labor that had since been traded in for efficiency and profit. After discussing the ideas of Ruskin and Carlyle, Morris and his friends began to view themselves as a medieval brotherhood, artistic and altruistic in nature, united by a hatred of the cold perfection of mechanical production and the profit motive in their own culture. For a model, Morris may have looked to the Apostles, a previous Oxford brotherhood that had counted the poets Browning and Tennyson among its members.

In the brotherhood's all-night conferences, Morris again displayed his propensity to dominate conversation for hours at a time, turning discussion into a rousing lecture. His friends seem to have delighted in his talk, finding his emotional intensity endearing and inspiring. He and his friends were emboldened by currents in English intellectual society, currents that ran counter to the trends of industrial mass production and middle class aspiration. All around them, religious and secular brotherhoods and communes proliferated in response to dehumanized urban environments and the dominance of commerce, the image of a degraded England that Morris had absorbed from reading Dickens as a boy. In reality, Morris's brotherhood was little more than a collegiate social clique bent on distinguishing themselves from their more typical and "barbaric" classmates, those middle class capitalists in training. Their righteous charade, however, proved to be an invaluable opportunity to form an aesthetic and to envision future goals, however misty and idealistic they might have been at the time.

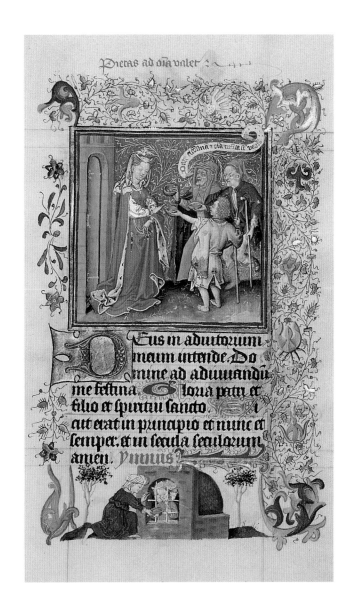

Piety: Lady Distributing Alms.
Unknown artist, c. 1435. Illumination from Book of Hours of Catherine of Cleves. *The Pierpont Morgan Library, New York.* Morris's lifelong interest in printing began with a fascination with illuminated manuscripts like this one. Later in life, he would collect old books, which he regarded as art works of the highest order. He also experimented with manuscript illumination himself.

FOLLOWING PAGE:
Peach Wallpaper
WILLIAM MORRIS, 1866; print design. Victoria & Albert Museum, London. Although Morris preferred tapestries and chintzes, wallpapers offered him the opportunity to make the firm's goods available to the less wealthy. *Peach* is one of Morris's first and most rudimentary wall-paper designs.

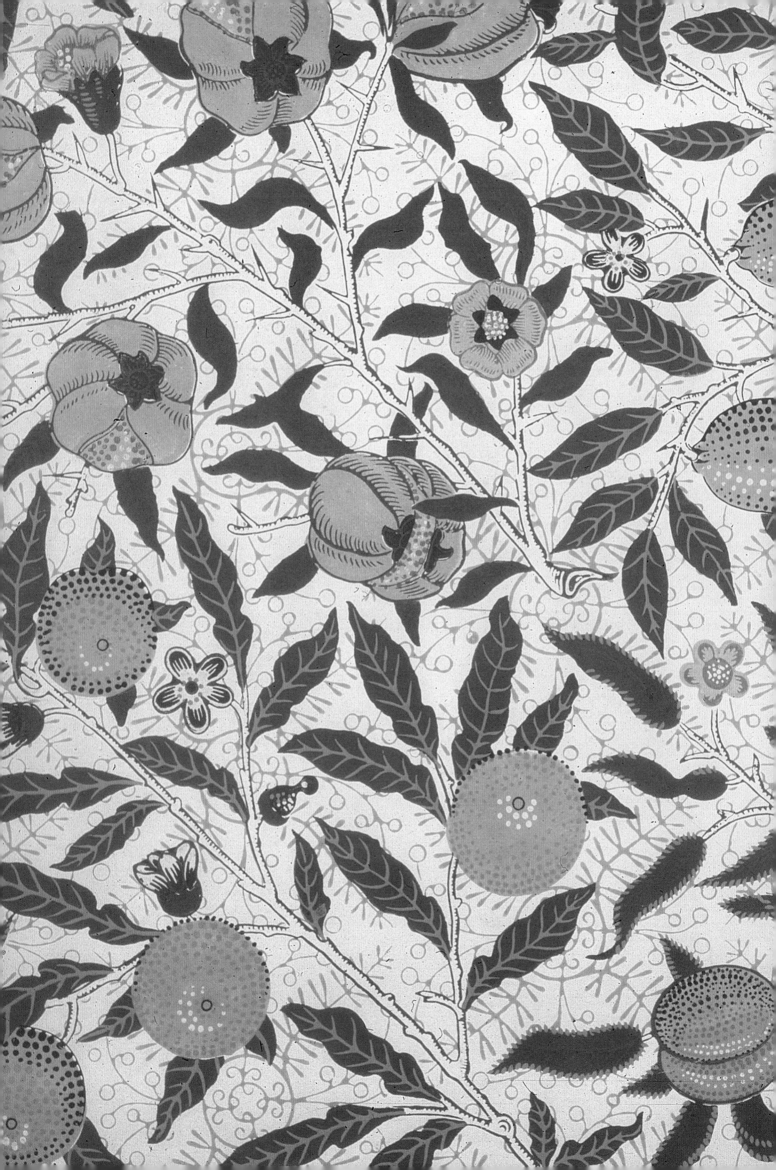

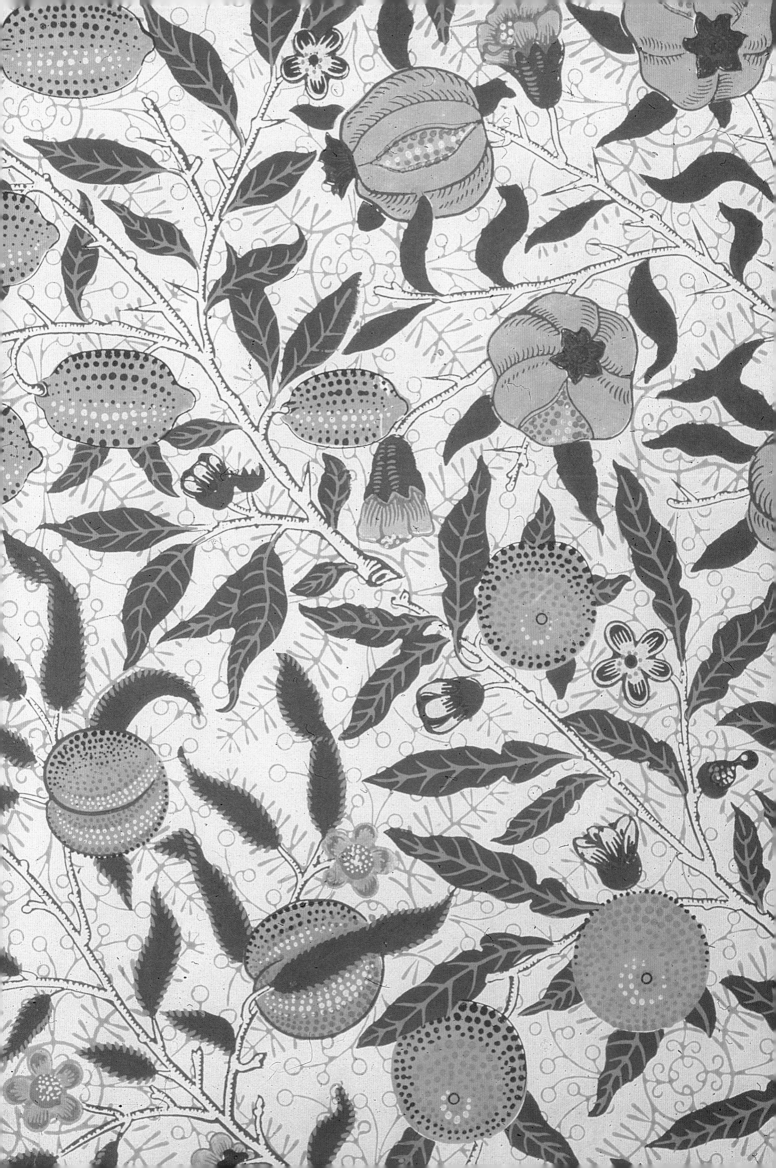

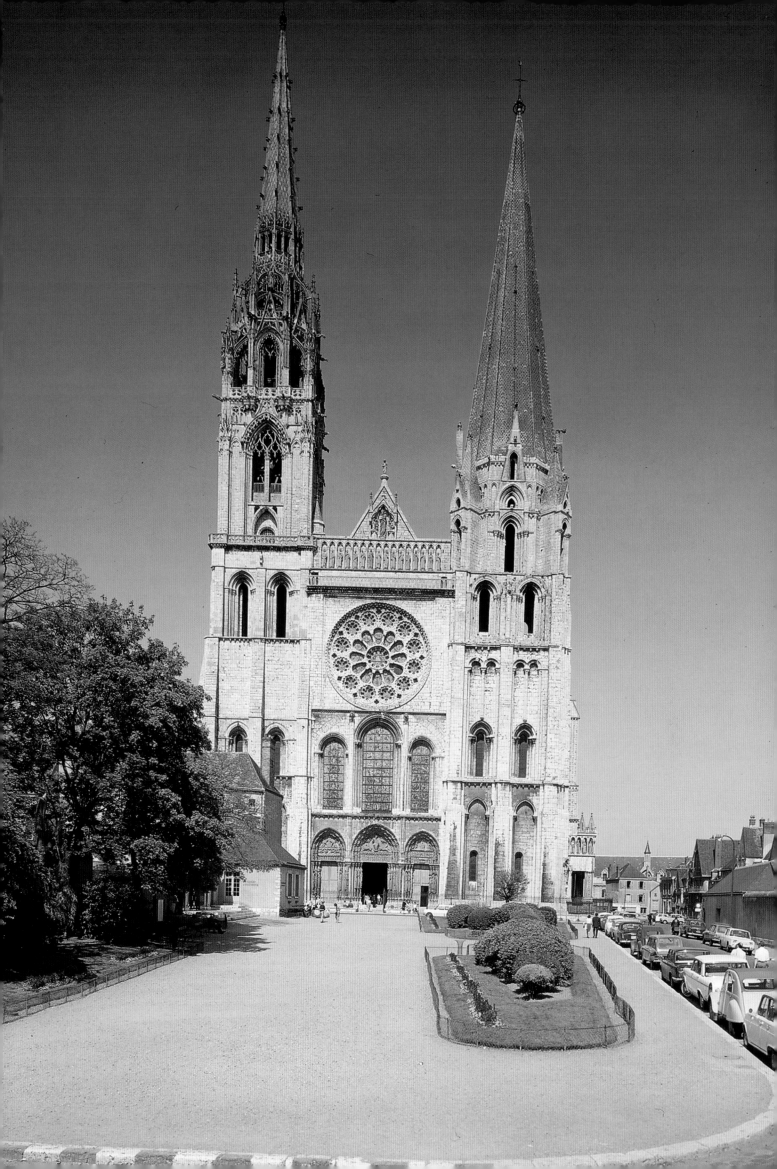

Rehearsals:
Morris Imagines his Future

Morris's artistic ambition was further fueled by a trip he and Burne-Jones took to northern France and Belgium in the Summer of 1854. In his letters and lectures, Morris frequently cited this tour as a turning point in his life, his first adult exposure to Flemish painting and to the Gothic cathedrals of Amiens, Rouen, and Chartres. Around this time, Morris and Burne-Jones also became aware of the Pre-Raphaelites, a brotherhood of controversial painters who were making waves in the art world in London, drawing even the attention of Morris's beloved John Ruskin. It would not be long before that brotherhood and Morris's own united, with Ruskin himself as a frequent visitor. Although neither Morris nor Burne-Jones could have imagined the connections and adventures that awaited them, it was becoming increasingly clear to both that art was their calling, a life devoted to the creation and perception of beauty. To what extent this would be compatible with their Church allegiance, still strong, was unclear.

In 1855, the brotherhood decided on a whim to publish a fledgling monthly review in which to showcase poetry and essays on art and architecture. Later described by Morris as "very young indeed," the *Oxford and Cambridge Magazine* lasted for a total of twelve issues. It was in these pages that Morris discovered, almost to his surprise, that he could write poetry. His short verses inspired by chivalric romances were a feature of each issue. It seems Morris never found writing verse difficult. In later years, he would compose poetry while he worked a loom or sketched a design, breaking frequently to record the rhymes he had collected in his head. Even when difficult social issues were to dominate his attention and efforts, Morris still produced abundant prose and verse romances, no doubt incarnations of the sword-clashing stories he had told himself as a child riding through the forest on his pony.

At first, Morris also served as the editor of the *Oxford and Cambridge Magazine* but soon turned

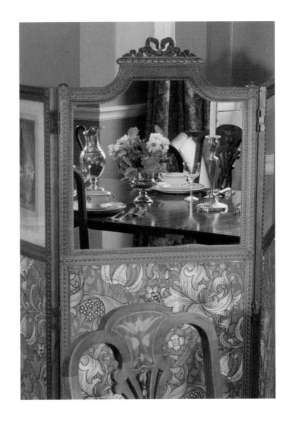

Screen with Morris design
Morris & Co., 1817. Regency House, Kent. Morris's designs were incorporated into a variety of Victorian furnishings. This screen, from an English Regency House, formerly a vicarage, is covered in one of Morris' popular textile designs.

those duties over to William Fulford. This would be typical of Morris's priorities. He had little patience for administrative or bureaucratic responsibilities. He had, moreover, no *need* to bother with such trivialities; at the age of twenty-one, Morris had come into an annual salary of £900 from the Devonshire copper mine shares. For comparison, the highest paid dons at Oxford at the time rarely earned more than £250 per year.

Morris, then, was not merely the mouth of the brotherhood; he was also the money. He subsidized the magazine and treated his less wealthy friends well, almost as if he were rewarding them for their interest and faith in him. With this large and reliable income always there to bolster him, Morris was on the verge of an extended period of experimentation, a period in which he would start and abandon careers, find his voice as a poet, and find that the Church no longer embodied his beliefs or accommodated his vision.

The brotherhood had declared, in Burne-Jones's words, "Holy Warfare against the age." In fact, Morris's actual commitment to social reform was many years and several careers

West Facade, Royal Portal
Cathedral, Chartres. When Burne-Jones and Morris journeyed to France in the Summer of 1854, They spent much of their time exploring and admiring Gothic Cathedrals such as the one at Chartres.

Guinevere

WILLIAM MORRIS,
1858; oil on canvas;
28¼ x 19¾ in.
(71.7 x 50.1 cm). The
Tate Gallery, London.
The themes and
characters of
Arthurian legend
were ever-present
in Morris's poetry
and, when he dared
to paint or otherwise
represent human
forms, in his art as
well. At the end
of his life, illness
forced Morris to
abandon plans for
a Kelscott Press
edition of Malory's
Morte d'Arthur.

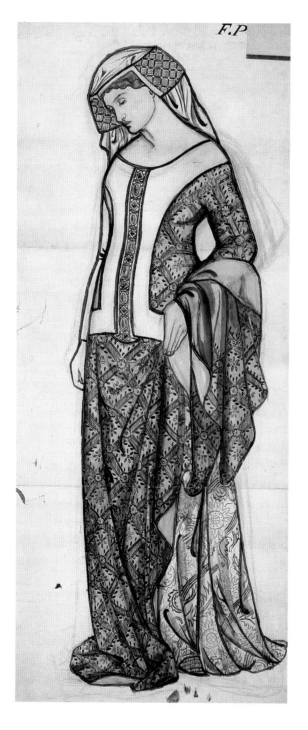

away. For now, he found his social conscience took a back seat to his passion for art. The holy warfare would have to wait. More pressing was the issue of his immediate future. Was he to continue along the path toward a Church career, or was his ever-increasing interest in art and architecture to have its way? Burne-Jones was already solemnly committed to becoming an artist. Morris doubted his own potential as a painter but felt reasonably confident that his abiding interest in old buildings qualified him for a career in architecture. So Morris followed suit, renouncing his intention of taking Holy Orders much to the chagrin of his mother. In a nearly desperate plea to win her approval, Morris composed a self-portrait of lasting truth:

> . . . You said then, you remember, and said very truly, that it was an evil thing to be an idle objectless man; I am fully determined not to incur this reproach . . . . An university education fits a man about as much for being a ship-captain as a Pastor of souls: besides your money has by no means been thrown away, if the love of friends faithful and true, friends first seen and loved here, if this love is something priceless, and not to be bought again anywhere and by any means: if moreover by living here and seeing evil and sin in its foulest and coarsest forms, as one does day by day, I have learned to hate any form of sin, and to wish to fight against it, is not this well too? . . . I am pretty confident I will succeed, and make I hope a decent architect sooner or later: and you know too that in any work one delights in, even the merest drudgery connected with it is delightful too.

He would never be anything like an idle or objectless man; the love of faithful friends would sustain him throughout his life; and, although he never became a practicing architect, the love of meaningful work, drudgery and all, best describes the essence of William Morris.

Pimpernel Wallpaper

WILLIAM MORRIS, 1876; print design. Victoria & Albert Museum, London.
One can assume that the *Pimpernel* wallpaper was
one of Morris's personal favorites; it adorned the walls
of the dining room at his Kelmscott Manor home.

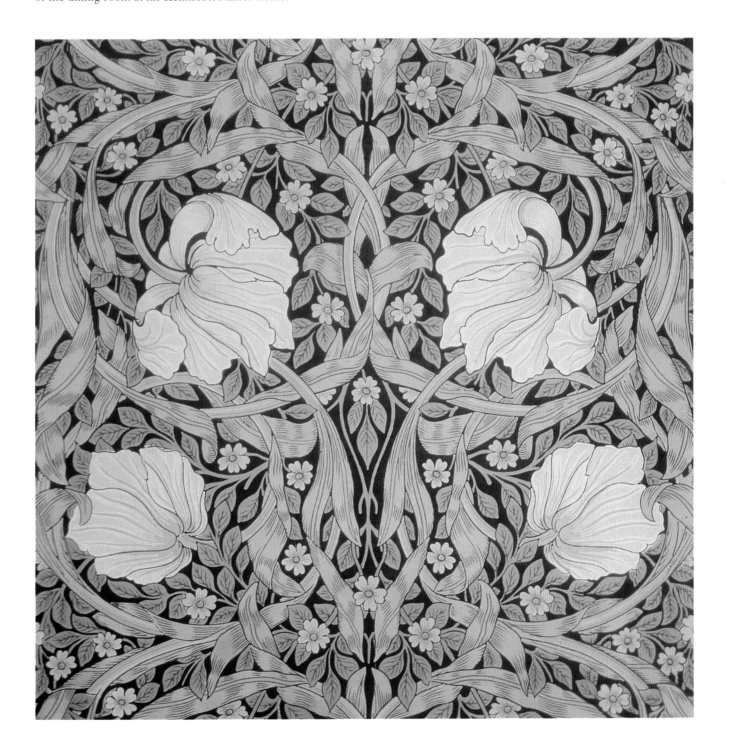

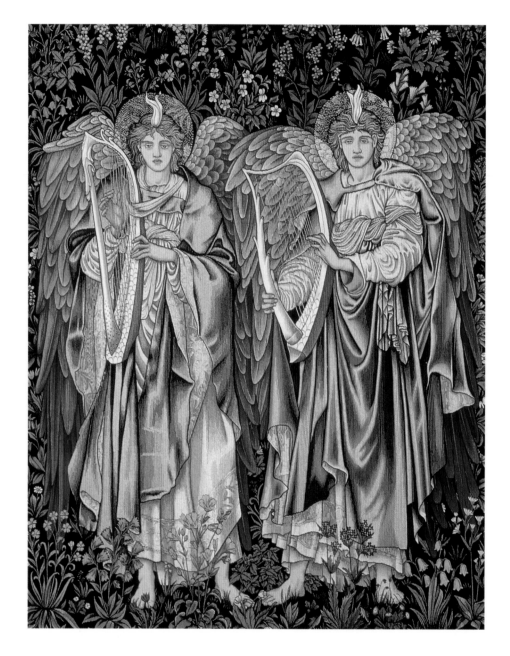

Angeli Laudantes

*WILLIAM MORRIS,
1894; tapestry in wool
and silks. Victoria &
Albert Museum, London.*
This popular tapestry
was taken from an
1878 stained-glass
window design for
Salisbury Cathedral
by Edward Burne-
Jones. The firm fre-
quently reused designs
in multiple media.
Angeli Laudantes and
its companion tapes-
try, *Angeli Minis-
trantes*, were in great
demand in churches
throughout England.

Evenlode

WILLIAM MORRIS, 1883; printed cotton. Victoria & Albert Museum, London.
Like most of Morris's later chintzes, *Evenlode* was printed at
the firm's Merton Abbey works. *Evenlode* was also the first
Morris design named after a tributary of the Thames.

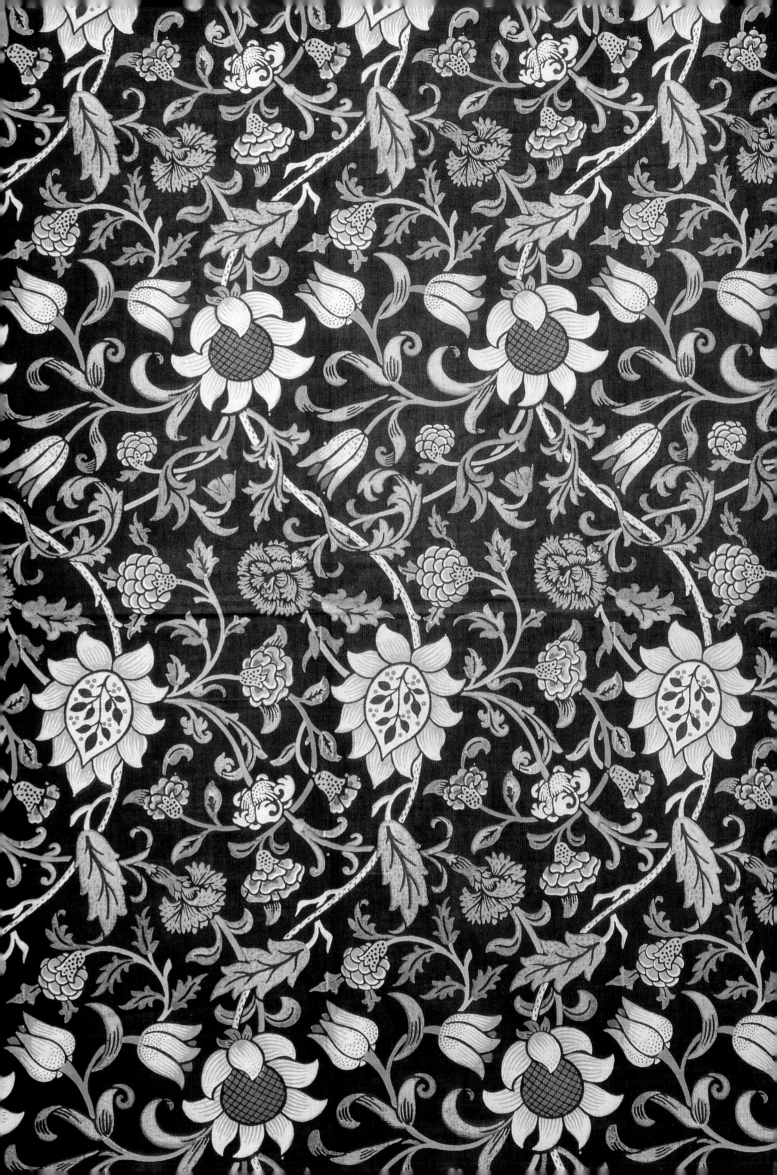

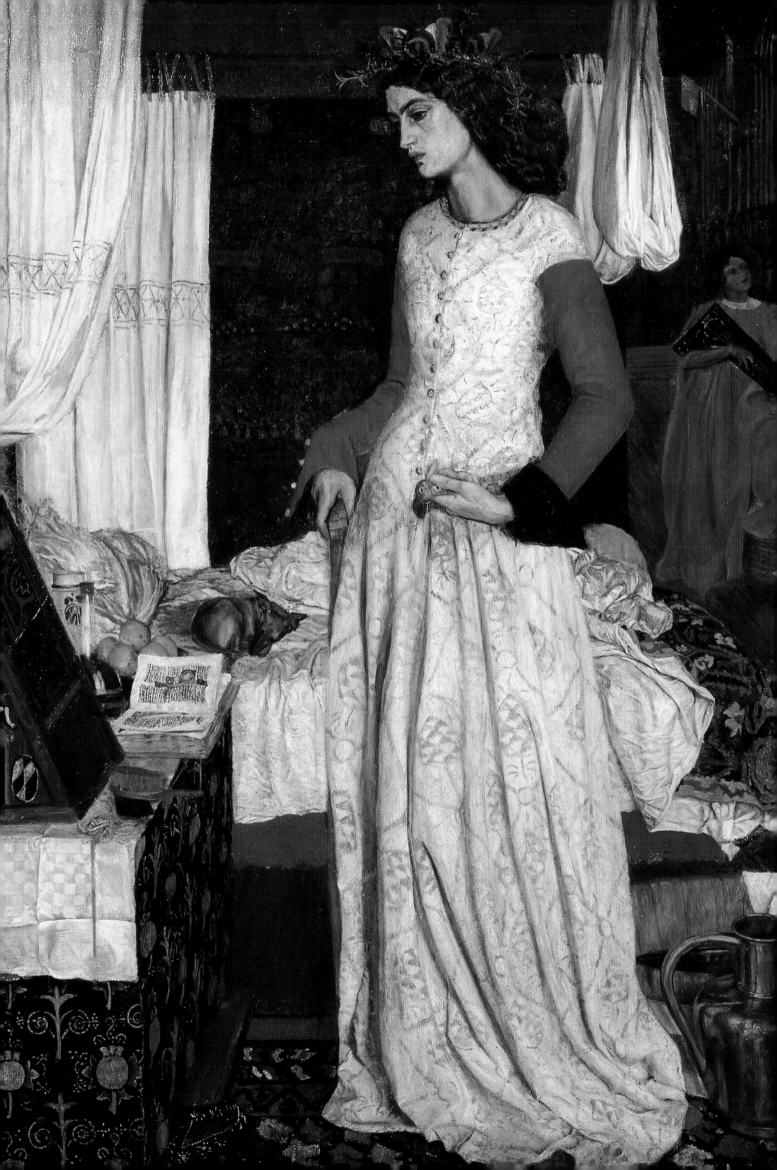

Chapter Two

TRANSITIONS: LONDON, ROSSETTI, AND THE RED HOUSE

Imagine a young man of independent and inexhaustible wealth; myriad interests, passions, and fascinations; and hearty appetites for food, drink, and the company of friends. Imagine him set loose at the end of his college years, alienated from his family and without a clear career direction. Such was the frightening and exhilarating position of William Morris when he was graduated from Oxford in the Autumn of 1855. Certainly, he faced a world of opportunity but also the prospects of aimlessness and squandering. Burne-Jones had left Oxford without taking a degree, committed to being a painter or nothing. Morris felt the need for a similarly singular and passionate focus, but none presented itself with any true conviction.

Should he become, like his friend, a painter? The notion occurred to him, but Morris knew in his bones that, while he could certainly labor to achieve competence, his painting would never be transcendent. Was he to be a poet? He had demonstrated a facility and ease with poetic language, but his output to date was meager and embryonic. Another kind of artist? Virtually all of the arts appealed to him, and his hunger to experiment, not to mention his leisure, was boundless. To appease his family and his conscience, though, he needed something definite,

something to call himself, an identity. Architecture won by default. He had the background to justify it and felt he had the ability to master it. Thus, Morris declared architecture to be his calling and his future. It would not be long before this pretense crumbled and Morris returned to his true vocation: finding an identity the expensive way, forging it from multiple identities, following every divergent impulse and interest until they cohered into a complex, multi-faceted whole.

Of all the architects redesigning England in the Gothic image at the time, the young G.E. Street was one of Morris's favorites. Street primarily designed churches, although his most famous work would be the Law Courts on the strand in London. Conveniently, Street had an office in Oxford. Shortly after graduation, Morris approached Street and requested an apprenticeship. He soon went to work in the office and found the environment pleasant and congenial. One of the other apprentices stuttered badly but was apparently able to sing without hesitation, so the group took to communicating with sing-song conversations through rolls of architect's paper. Although his heart was never solidly committed to architecture, Morris found Street to be a useful and

Queen Guinevere or La Belle Iseult

WILLIAM MORRIS, 1858; oil on canvas; 28½ x 20 in. (71.1 x 50.8 cm). The Tate Gallery, London. One of Morris's few surviving paintings, *Queen Guinevere or La Belle Iseult* is considered significant chiefly as evidence of Morris's lack of facility with the human form. It also demonstrates the extent to which Arthurian legend penetrated his personal life.

William Morris and Edward Burne-Jones in the garden of the Grange, Fulham

1874; photograph by Frederick Hollyer. The Hulton Getty Picture Collection Limited. Lifelong friends and collaborators, Morris and Burne-Jones could not have been more different in disposition. The quiet and reflective Burne-Jones lovingly poked fun at Morris's famous temper and hearty appetites in many cartoons and caricatures.

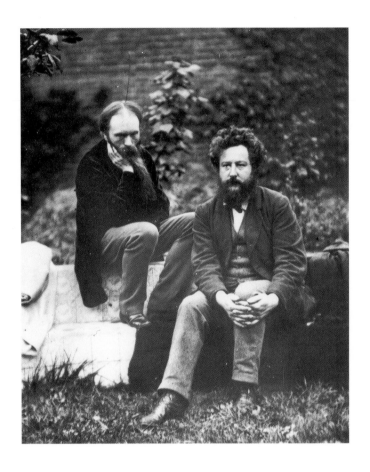

Queen Guinevere or La Belle Iseult

detail; WILLIAM MORRIS, 1858; oil on canvas; 28½ x 20 in. (71.1 x 50.8 cm). The Tate Gallery, London. Jane Morris posed for Morris' one surviving oil painting, *Guenevere or La Belle Isuelt*, a work best known as evidence of Morris's clumsiness at figure painting. He is reported to have written on its back, "I cannot paint you, but I love you."

in Canterbury, a beneficial exercise in discipline and particularity, to be sure, but hardly the kind of grand artistic endeavor that he felt himself cut out for. Years later, he would question the validity and wisdom of Street's Gothic revivals. Like Ruskin, he would come to see art and architecture as direct expressions of a particular society and lament the attempt to recapture an era simply by mimicking its buildings.

Judgments like this, however, were not on Morris's mind when he made the decision to abandon architecture and throw himself back into a period of uncertainty and possibility. Burne-Jones had left Oxford and moved to London where he was studying and socializing with the Pre-Raphaelites. Morris observed their lifestyle on frequent weekend visits and liked what he saw. With his best friend already established there, Morris followed to find himself new mentors. What he would learn in London was less a skill than an attitude that would lead him to master many skills.

willing mentor. Street taught as much to Morris on a summer trip to southern Europe as he did around the office. More significantly, at Street's office Morris met Philip Webb, whom he would call the best man he had ever known. Three years Morris's senior, Webb would become one of the most prominent designers at Morris's firm and, of all his close friends, the only one to follow him politically when he turned to socialism.

Morris spent nine months as Street's apprentice, and though the experience was quite useful in several ways, his excitement steadily dwindled. Perhaps this had something to do with the assignments Street gave him. Morris spent most of his time meticulously copying a drawing of a single doorway at St. Augustine's

The Spell of Rossetti

Although history sometimes regards William Morris and Edward Burne-Jones as late Pre-Raphaelites, this is somewhat misleading. By the time Morris moved permanently to London, the Pre-Raphaelite Brotherhood had more or less dissolved, or had at least been exposed. While its principal members continued successful careers in painting, the excitement and controversy of their challenge to the artistic mainstream had waned; they were on the verge of becoming old news. It is more accurate to say

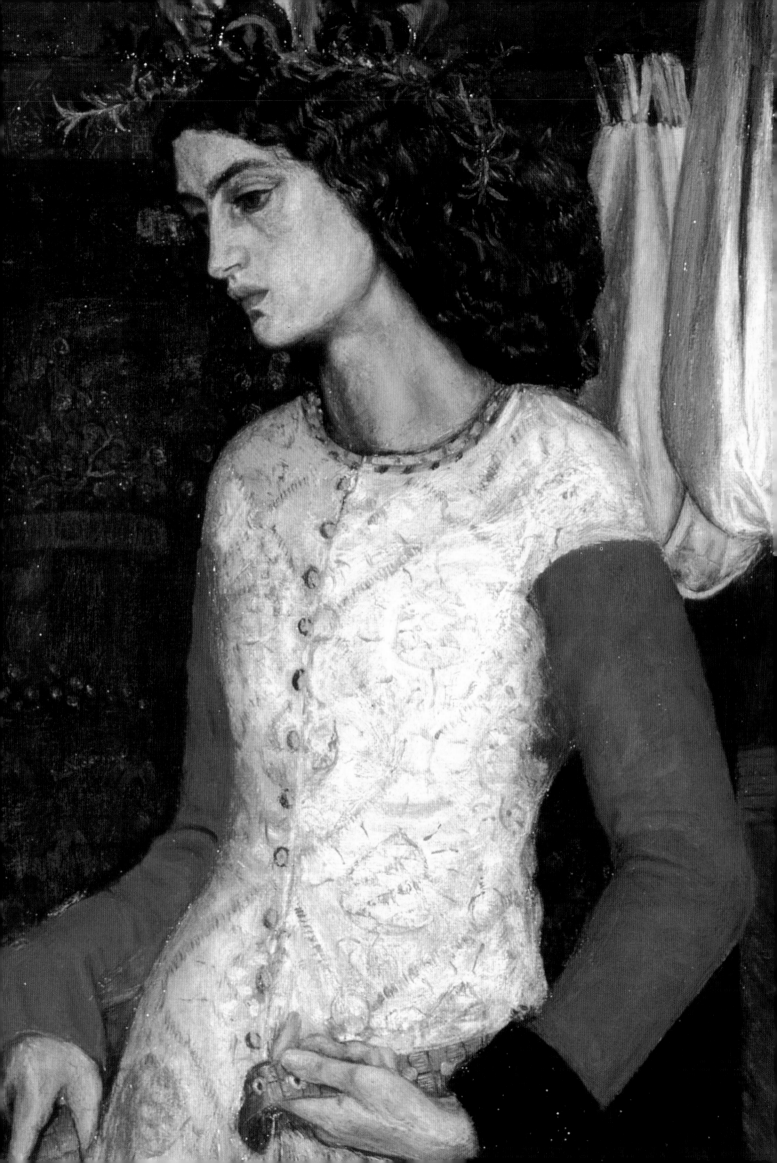

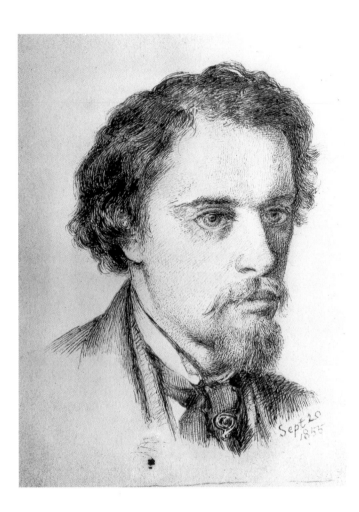

Self-Portrait

Dante Gabriel Rossetti,
1855; drawing; William
Morris Gallery, London.
Rossetti was instru-
mental in Morris's
exploration of his tal-
ents. Without Ros-
setti's guidance and
encouragement, Mor-
ris might well have
ended up the "decent
architect" that he
promised his mother
he would become.

perfection of the Renaissance master Raphael, whose work, at the
time, was considered the academic
standard of taste. The Pre-
Raphaelites adorned their paintings with the cryptic initials P.R.B.
(for theirs was, at first, a secret
brotherhood). Their short-lived
magazine, *The Germ*, had provided
the model for the *Oxford and Cam-*
bridge Magazine. They shared a
common pool of influences with
Morris: Malory's *Morte d'Arthur*
and other chivalric romances, Romantic poetry, Ruskin, and medieval art. Although Rossetti was
only six years older than Morris,
he was already a painter and poet
of reputation. Morris regarded
him simply as "a very great man."

The Pre-Raphaelite credo of
passion, as embodied by Rossetti,
extended beyond art. Rossetti was
playful, wild, lusty, and afflicted
with what today might be called a
bi-polar disorder characterized by
unpredictable mood swings and a
deep streak of melancholy. His mercurial
behavior steadily alienated his friends and fol-
lowers (including Morris some twenty years
later), but in the mid-1850s he was at the height
of his creative powers and charisma. He introduced Morris and Burne-Jones to London bo-
hemia, and taught them the style as well as the
substance of a revolutionary artist. Perhaps in-
hibited by the echoes of his evangelical upbringing, or perhaps because of an idealized
romanticism, Morris did not take part in the
Pre-Raphaelite's famed sexual exploits, but in all
other respects he embraced the loose and care-
free lifestyle of Rossetti. He let his beard and
hair grow into tangled locks, ate and drank

that Morris and Burne-Jones, impressionable
and idealistic artists that they were, went to
London to take life lessons from the Pre-
Raphaelite's most famous, charismatic, and
dangerous brother, Dante Gabriel Rossetti.

If Morris and Burne-Jones had played make-
believe at Oxford, fancying themselves a brotherhood while tucked away safely in the ivory
tower, then Rossetti was the real thing. Along
with the painters John Everett Millais, William
Holman Hunt, and Ford Maddox Brown, Rossetti had formed the Pre-Raphaelite Brotherhood in 1848. Their name, coined by Hunt and
rued by their defender Ruskin, referred to their
rejection of the muted emotion and cold

prodigiously, and, under Rossetti's tutelage, assumed the imposing and unruly appearance for which he would become famous.

Emphatically apolitical, Rossetti influenced Morris to silence his bothersome social conscience and embrace an aesthetic, art for art's sake philosophy. Under Rossetti's spell, Morris wrote in 1856, "I can't enter into politico-social subjects with any interest . . . I have no power or vocation to set them right in ever so little a degree. My work is the embodiment of dreams in one form or another." Rossetti prodded Morris to indulge every creative whim and fancy, and Morris was soon painting, illuminating manuscripts, experimenting with embroidery, and composing the poems that would eventually form *The Defence of Guenevere*. For the rooms he shared with Burne-Jones at Red Lion Square, Morris designed striking medieval furniture, including a large and heavy settle with panels painted by Rossetti. Rossetti said of the Red Lion Square decoration project, "Morris is rather doing the magnificent there." Emboldened by Rossetti's friendship and encouragement, Morris adopted a personal motto from the painter Van Eyck: *Als ich kanne*, if I can. In most artistic endeavors, he could.

In 1857, Rossetti organized his new hybrid brotherhood to paint frescoes on the walls of the new Debating Hall at Oxford. It was for Morris a triumphant homecoming to his alma mater in the company of one of the age's most controversial and flamboyant figures. Burne-Jones remembered it as a summer of high-spirited and jubilant artistic terrorism, full of practical jokes, flirtation, and

passionate painting. In one famous episode, Topsy, as Morris came to be known, got his head caught in the visor of a suit of armor and staggered around cursing, much to the amusement of his companions. Perhaps the atmosphere was too frivolous in one respect; the artists failed to properly prime the brick facades on which the frescoes were painted, and their scenes from *Morte d'Arthur* began disappearing almost as soon as they were completed. Morris attempted to restore the work almost twenty years later but was unsuccessful; the famous, and invisible, collaboration would live on only in legend.

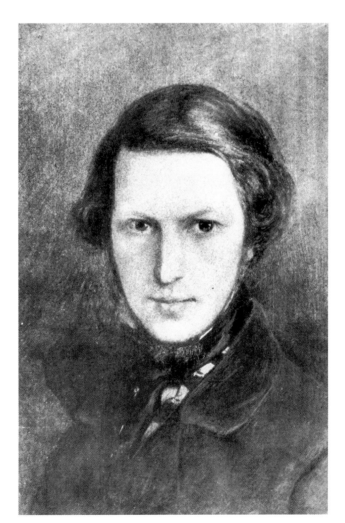

Self-Portrait
FORD MADOX BROWN,
1850. Corbis-Bettmann.
Madox Brown was a leading Pre-Raphaelite painter and one of the founding members of Morris, Marshall, Faulkner & Co. Brown's work for the firm is significant but scant. He devoted most of his time to his painting career.

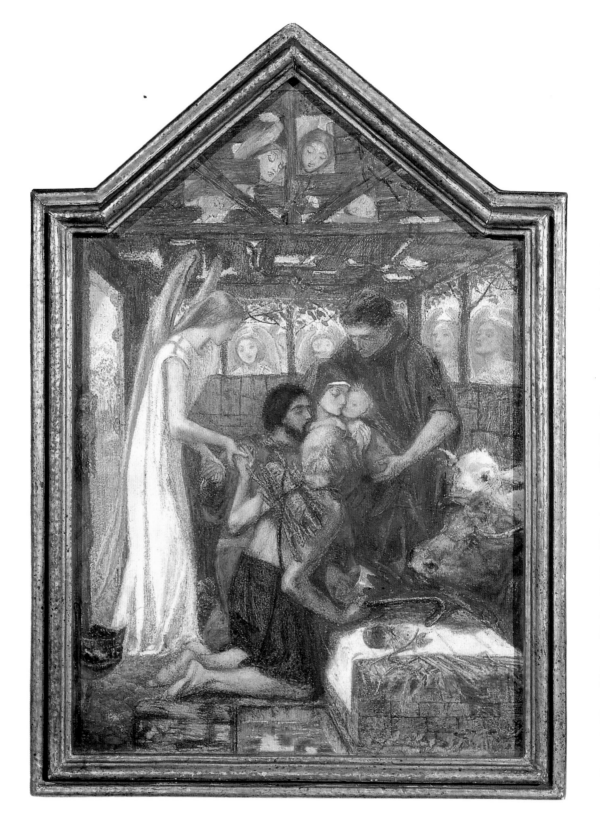

**The Seed
of David**

*DANTE GABRIEL
ROSSETTI, 1858–64;
oil on wood; center
panel of a triptych
altarpiece, 90 x 60 in
(228.6 x 152.5 cm.).
Tate Gallery, London.*
Rossetti's and Morris's
lives intertwined in
a myriad of ways,
from their artistic en-
deavors to Rossetti's
later affair with Jane.
Rossetti used both
Morris and Jane
as models for this
triptych altarpiece.

A Stunner

Topsy Morris, hirsute, disheveled, and prone to emotional outbursts, hardly fit the classic image of the sensitive poet and artist. The poet whose perennial themes were unrequited love and infidelity looked more the part of a hearty sailor. It seemed he had loved only two women: his mother and his oldest sister, both named Emma. He was inexperienced at love and almost certainly possessed an idealized notion of romance, shaped by the art and liter-ature of chivalry. He could imagine himself paying tribute and singing praises in art and verse; whether he had any awareness of the reality of relationships and compatibility is another question.

On a night at the theater in 1857, Rossetti and Burne-Jones directed Morris's attention to a particular "stunner," as they called attractive women, seated in the row behind them. Her pale face, fine and delicate bone structure, black hair, and long, slender neck were the very definition of Pre-Raphaelite beauty. Rossetti, already involved with, and soon to be engaged to, Elizabeth Siddal, goaded Morris to approach seventeen year old Jane Burden. If Rossetti was not at liberty to pursue Burden, then he would at least have her in his circle. Morris more than willingly obliged, as if Rossetti's interest deemed her a suitable mate. It was to be Rossetti's most mixed and ambiguous contribution to Morris's life, and, ultimately, the cause of their falling out.

Morris and Burden would make a strangely mismatched couple. She was the daughter of a stable-hand, he the son of a wealthy capitalist. But class was the least significant of their differences. Jane Burden Morris was as quiet and mysterious as Morris was loquacious and transparent. Their awkward courtship consisted of Morris's lengthy recitations of verse, sometimes his own, sometimes the classics. Years later, Rossetti satirized their unlikely marriage in a cartoon. The robust Morris is shown reciting from numbered volumes of his long poem *The Earthly Paradise*, while Jane lies tortured in the bathtub next to a line of numbered empty spa-water glasses, one for each volume of the poem. With one becoming famous for her silence and the other for his noise, their marriage would produce two children, survive ill-health and infidelity, and remain intact until Morris's death.

Love, however, was the one quiet tragedy of Morris's life. In April 1859 he married the woman whom Rossetti would immortalize in paint and Henry James in words: ". . . an apparition of fearful and wonderful intensity. It's hard to say whether she's a grand synthesis of all the Pre-Raphaelite pictures ever made—

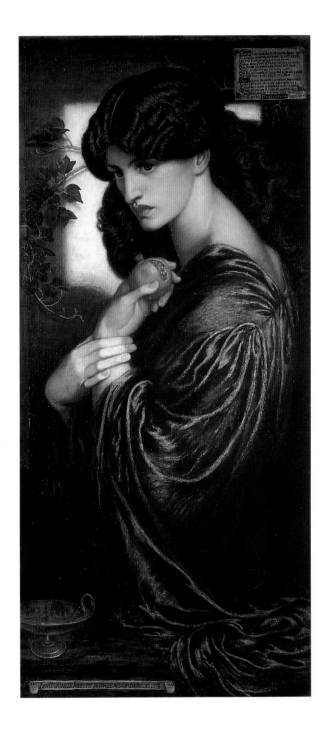

Prosperine

DANTE GABRIEL ROSSETTI, 1874; oil on canvas;
49³/₄ x 24 in. (126.4 61 cm). The Tate Gallery, London.
Jane Morris posed as Prosperine, the captive wife of a God. Rossetti might have imagined Janey to be in such a position herself. She posed for a number of Rossetti's paintings, and there is little doubt that he fell in love with her after his own wife, Elizabeth Siddal, committed suicide.

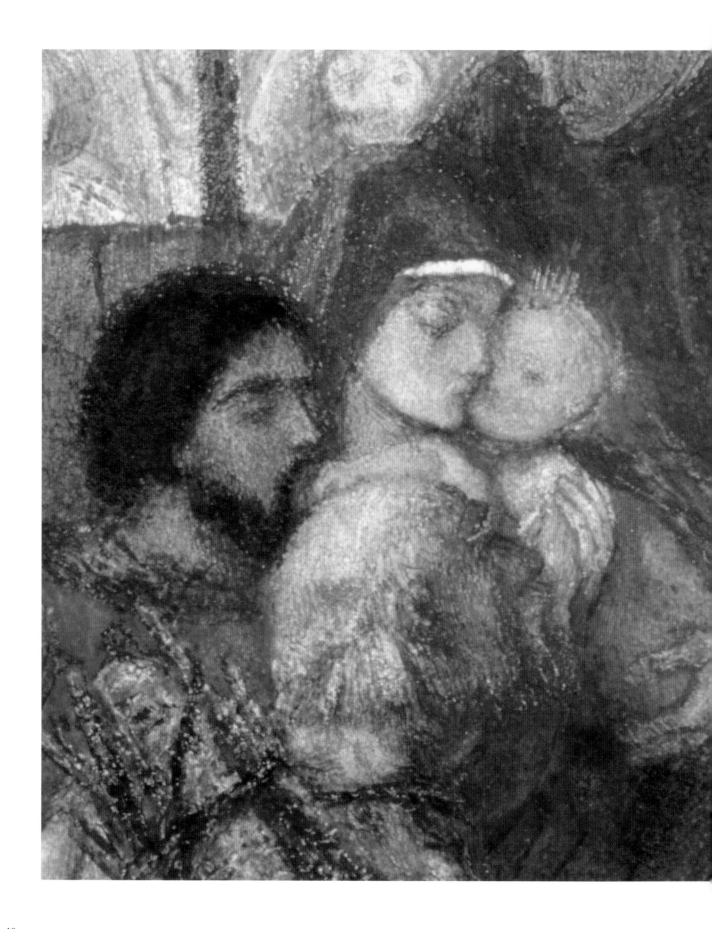

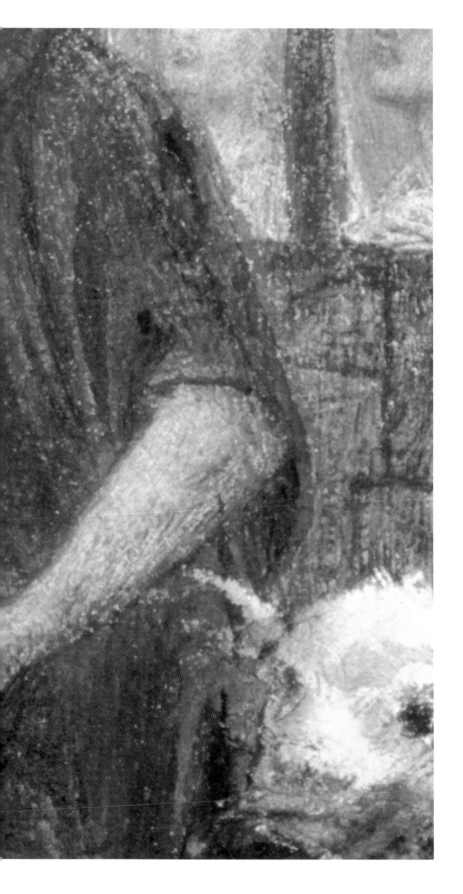

or they a 'keen analysis' of her . . . ." Morris's own artistic tributes to her were less successful. She posed for his one surviving oil painting, *Guenevere* or *La Belle Isuelt*, a work best known as evidence of Morris's clumsiness at figure painting. He is reported to have written on its back, "I cannot paint you, but I love you." In his many acclaimed paintings of Jane, Rossetti endowed her with a distant, difficult sexuality and buried passion that Morris had difficulty accessing as an artist and as a husband. Rossetti would taste that passion, when, after years of implicit and sublimated courtship, he and Jane had an affair in the 1870s. Morris knew full well what was transpiring, and in a decision that must have anguished him, fled to Iceland and left the lovers alone in his Kelmscott Manor home for the better part of two years. He lived quietly with the knowledge of the betrayal, as if deferring one last time to the higher master.

The Seed of David
detail; DANTE GABRIEL ROSSETTI, 1858–64;
oil on wood; center panel of a triptych altarpiece,
90 x 60 in (228.6 x 152.5 cm.). Tate Gallery, London.
In this triptych celebrating the birth of Christ, Rossetti used both Morris and Jane Burden as models. Rossetti used the young, still delicate features of Morris for the head of David.

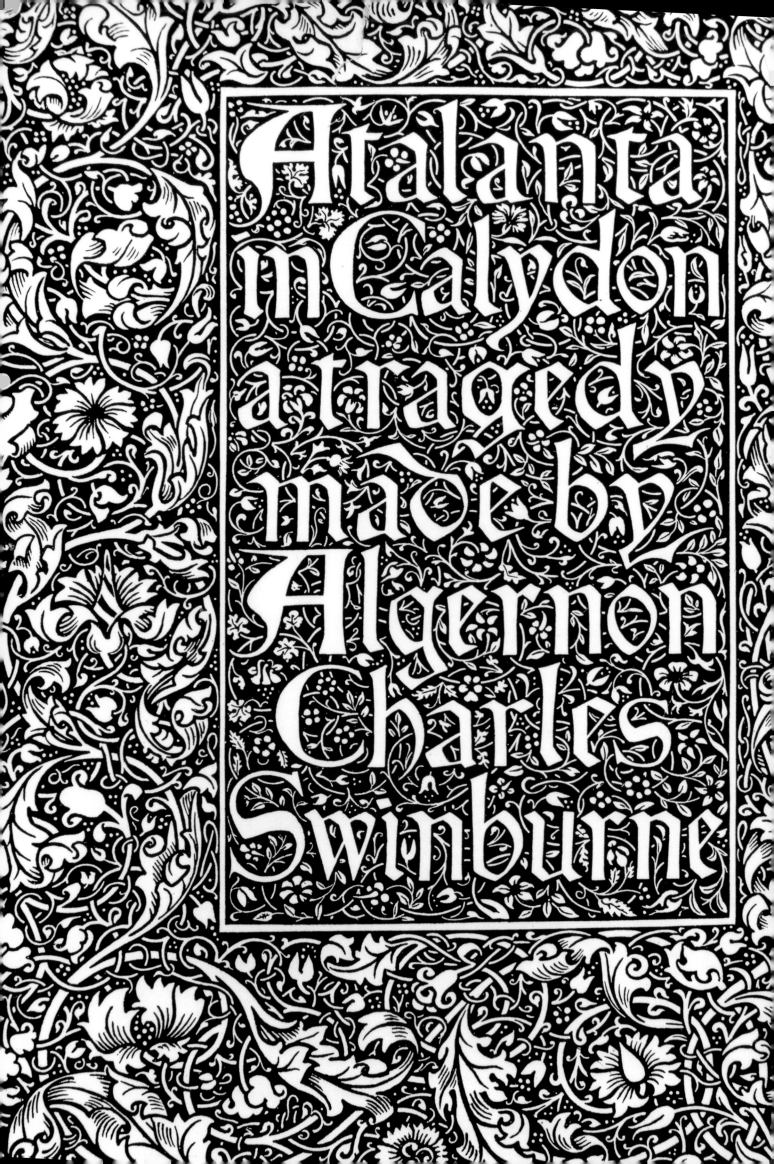

Atalanta in Calydon a tragedy made by Algernon Charles Swinburne

The Defence of Guenevere

Defence of Guenevere . . . is the most wonderful reproduction of the tone of thought
and feeling of a past age that has ever been
achieved.

J.H. SHORTHOUSE, *1859*

Disposed, as we are, to recognize all who
cultivate poetry honestly, whatever be the
style;—and admitting that Mr. Morris may
be counted among that choir,—we must
call attention to his book of Pre-Raphaelite
minstrelsy as to a curiosity which shows
how far affectation may mislead an earnest
man towards the fog-land of Art.

H.F. CHORLEY, *in* Athenaeum, *April 1858*

. . . we do not hesitate to pronounce that
if he do but wield the brush to half as much
purpose as the pen, his must be pictures
well worth a long pilgrimage to see.

RICHARD GARNETT,
Literary Gazette, *March 1858*

There are peculiarities both of thought and
style in this volume which will not escape
hostile criticism, but, in our judgment, it
contains ample proof of the author's title to
the privileges of a poet.

Unsigned review, Tablet, *April 1858*

Morris's first published collection of poems, *The Defence of Guenevere*, compressed the ever pop-ular Arthurian legends into short, lyrical verse. Equal parts romance and battle, the poems were a distillation of the imagery and narratives that had dominated Morris's artistic imagination for years, though he almost certainly intended them to be love poems to Jane as well. In retro-spect, Morris's defense of Guenevere's infidelity seems autobiographically prophetic. Jane would

play Guenevere to Rossetti's Lancelot. Morris, however, would not pursue vengeance as Arthur did, opting instead for conciliation and acquies-cence, a defense of human weakness. Amidst his lyrical narratives of lost love, combat, and death, Morris offered perhaps his most striking portrait of Jane in any media:

My lady seems of ivory
Forehead, straight nose, and cheeks that be
hollow'd a little mournfully;
Beata mea Domina!

The mixed reception received by the volume may have had something to do with Morris's af-filiation with the controversial Pre-Raphaelites, whose earnest passion was often mocked and mimicked. At the time, of course, Morris was unknown but for that connection. Whether dis-couraged by the lukewarm response or not (probably not), Morris would publish no more poetry until *The Life and Death of Jason* in 1867, followed immediately by the first volume of his most famous poetic work, *The Earthly Paradise*.

As a poet, Morris may best be described as pleasant and slightly melancholic, entranced by the legends and myths of the past, unencum-bered by irony, ambiguity, and any other ear-mark of modern poetry. To modern ears, he often sounds antiquated and quaint, but in his own time his idealistic worlds, be they medieval pasts or socialist futures, were much beloved di-versions and escapes. The self described "idle singer of an empty day" was highly regarded by such prominent contemporaries as Algernon Charles Swinburne and Oscar Wilde, and praised and consciously imitated by the great poet William Butler Yeats.

In spite of his respectable literary reputation (most poetry anthologies still reserve a few pages for him), Morris would do his most influ-ential and lasting work in other media. Poetry

Wood engraving for Swinburne's Atalanta in Caly-don—A Tragedy

WILLIAM MORRIS, n.d.; The Hulton Getty Picture Collection Limited. Morris and Swinburne met through their association with the Pre-Raphaelites and maintained a close literary friendship until Morris's death. Secretly, however, they often criticized each other's work. Morris found much of Swinburne's verse meek and over-wrought. Swinburne despised Morris's Icelandic sagas.

seems to have been therapy for him, a stream of lovesick and yearning song that might do him harm if left bottled up. By all accounts, he composed with remarkable ease; his verses seemingly bear no signs of labor. In most cases, such spontaneous fluidity is a hard-earned effect, not an accurate description of the composing process, as Yeats explained in "Adam's Curse":

> I said "A line will take us hours maybe;
> Yet if it does not seem a moment's thought,
> Our stitching and unstitching has been
>   naught."

But, while Morris certainly did revise conscientiously, rhymes seemed to come as easily to him as breathing. However, after the publication of *The Defence of Guenevere*, Morris put poetry on indefinite hold and turned his energies toward design and decoration. In the process of building and decorating his new home, the famous Red House, Morris would develop a philosophy of functionalism that would, in time, revolutionize English taste.

**William
Butler Yeats**

*Undated archival photograph;
UPI/Corbis-Bettmann.*
The young Irish poet
W. B. Yeats was a frequent visitor at Kelmscott in Morris's later years. In his autobiography, he wrote of Morris,
". . . whatever he pleased he did with an unheard-of ease and simplicity."
Yeats remembered Morris's late prose romances as "the only books I was ever to read slowly that I might not come too quickly to the end."

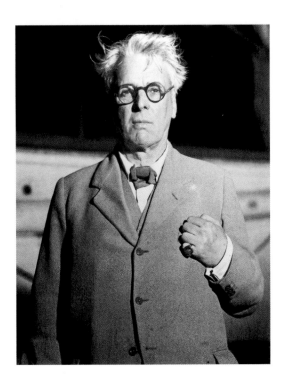

The Red House

The rooms that Morris shared with Burne-Jones at Red Lion Square were a quintessential artist's bachelor pad: messy, chaotic, wine-soaked, and littered with art supplies, tools, and half-finished furniture. They had served Morris well, once again making him the default host of the thriving young art scene. On a typical evening Morris would recite his poems at Rossetti's request, while other guests drank and talked and Burne-Jones quietly sketched the goings-on. Midnight visitors and drunken wee-hour banquets, however, were destined to end when Morris married Jane in 1859 and Burne-Jones followed him into matrimony a year later. Morris soon set out to design and build his dream house, putting his great financial resources behind the project and capitalizing on the diverse talents of his ever-growing circle of artist friends.

Morris had purchased a lot outside of London in Upton, now Bexleyheath, and the land served as a magnificent blank canvas for he and his companions. The Red House, so called because of its brick facade, would prove to be more than a new, spacious place to live. Many experts argue that its plainness and its implicit rejection of Victorian ostentation signify the beginning of modern architecture. More importantly at the time, the project motivated Morris and his friends to clarify their vision and put it into action. For all their talent and talk of changing the world, they had as yet produced very little as a group. The success of the Red House project taught Morris that the do-it-yourself ethic of the brotherhood could work on a large scale, that those despised, ornamental conventions of Victorian decor could be resisted, and a viable alternative demonstrated, simply through the passionate collaboration of enthusiastic amateurs. In this way, the Red House marked the beginning of the collaborative enterprise that would become Morris's firm. In the design and construction of his new abode, Morris finally discovered the focus and

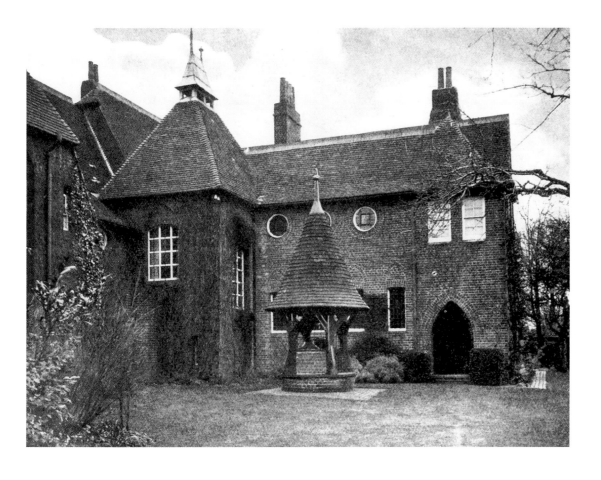

**The Red
House in Kent**

*The Hulton Getty
Picture Collection Limited.*
Designed in 1860 by
Philip Webb and dec-
orated by all the artists
who would become
the firm, the Red
House afforded Mor-
ris the opportunity
to put his beliefs into
action. Its medieval
character stood in
sharp contrast to the
dominant styles of
Victorian architecture
and demonstrated
a philosophy of
functionality that
would greatly influ-
ence twentieth-
century architecture.

purpose that were to dominate the next two decades of his life.

Morris knew better than to design the house himself. He knew enough about architecture to know what he wanted and what was feasible, but for actual plans, he turned to Philip Webb, his old companion from G.E. Street's office. In keeping with Morris's desire for a medieval house, Webb designed a two-story, L-shaped structure that resembled a monastery more than it did the palatial mansions of the day. In all phases of design and decoration, the men kept the principles of simplicity and functionality in mind. They chose red brick for the facade because it was plentiful in the region, unlike more popular exterior materials such as stone and stucco. The floors were made of tile. The simple staircases eschewed fashionable embell-ishments. For furnishings, Morris decided, as

usual, that what was commercially available simply wouldn't do. Several pieces of his own design were brought in from Red Lion Square, and the rest were designed and built by Morris and his friends. When the house was up and running, Rossetti, ever the arbiter of taste, de-clared the Red House to be ". . . more a poem than a house."

Decorating the house became a joyous and social process. Upon entering, visitors were handed paint brushes and instructed to decorate panels as they saw fit. In general, the jovial at-mosphere of Red Lion Square had simply moved up in the world. But the Red House has proven to be historically significant in several ways. First, it was Philip Webb's first major ar-chitectural project, and Webb would go on to become an important, but not prolific, archi-tect. Secondly, out of necessity, Morris further developed and refined his skills in a variety of media, most notably in the design of the tapestries and carpets that graced the Red House in plenitude. Finally, by deigning to concern themselves with furniture and decor, the high-minded aesthetes of the Pre-Raphaelite movement were implicitly arguing that the functional arts were high arts, worthy of the attention of serious artists. Thus, they established the central mission of the firm: a marriage of utility and serious artistic intent.

Briefly, Morris imagined that Red House might become the site of an experiment in communal living. If communal effort had produced it, why not take the enterprise one step further and fully realize the most profound ideals of brotherhood? Edward and Georgiana Burne-Jones were invited to live with the Morrises, and, after some serious consideration, declined. Morris was shaken by the rejection at first, but soon came to understand communal living as an idea whose time had not yet come, at least not for him. Meanwhile, the artistic collaboration continued in the direction of a more conventional business, one through which Morris would revolutionize household decor and attempt, from the living room out, to revolutionize the basis of society.

The Morris and Burne-Jones children at the Grange, Fulham

1874; photograph by Frederick Hollyer. The Hulton Getty Picture Collection Limited. Morris's first daughter, Jenny, suffered from epilepsy and never married. His second, May, followed her father into design and into socialism. She was married, briefly, to the socialist Henry Halliday Sparling and would dedicate much of her adult life to writing a biography of her father.

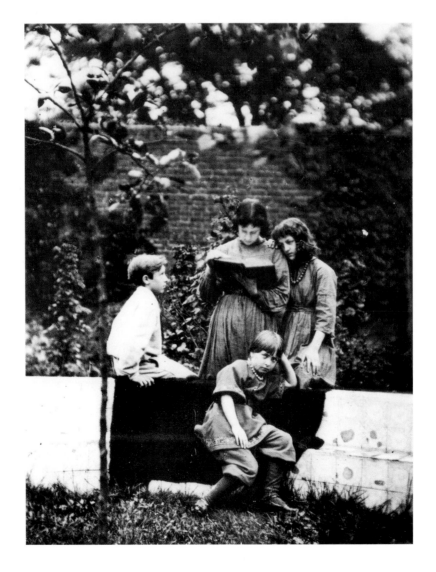

Daisy Wallpaper

WILLIAM MORRIS, 1864; Victoria & Albert Museum, London. Daisy was one of Morris's first wall-paper designs and the among the most popular ever produced by the firm. The pattern bears a striking resemblance to a hanging designed by Janey Morris for the Red House.

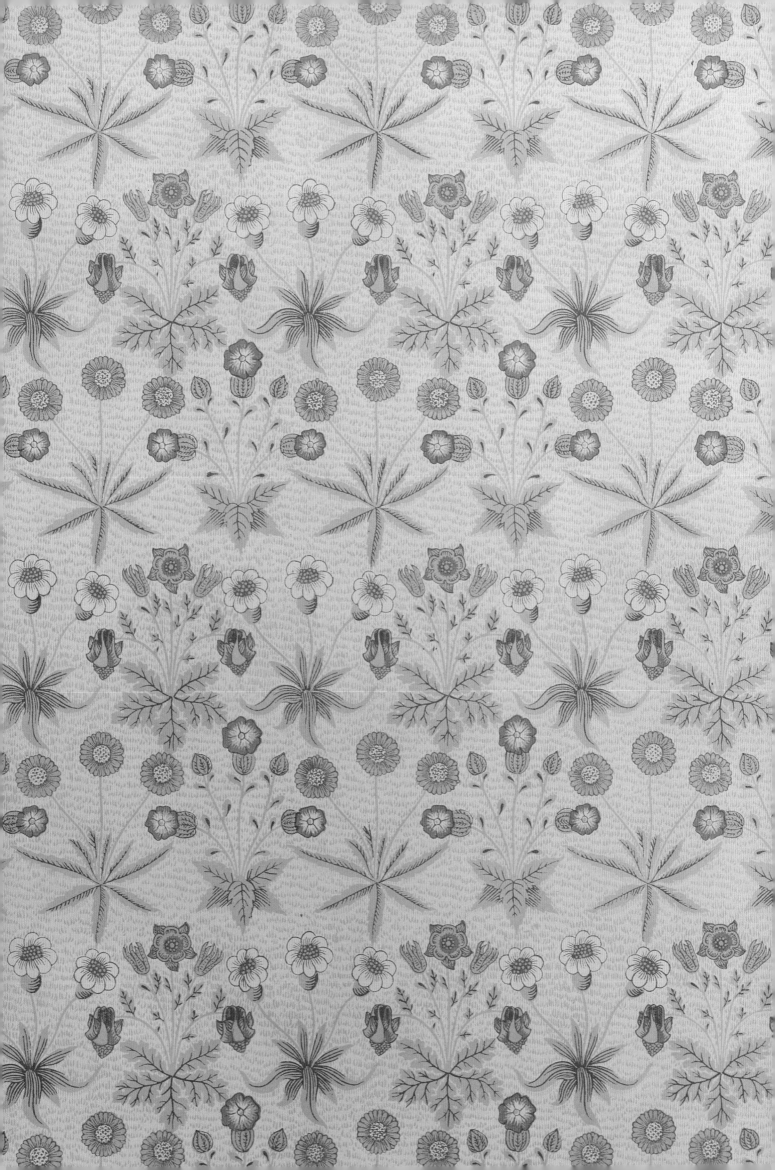

The Morris Chair

Designed by Philip Webb, c.1865;
William Morris Gallery, London.
This adjustable-back reclining chair is one of several pieces sometimes called the "Morris chair." Morris's physical comfort and stability were often the standards by the which the firm's products were judged. This particular chair is upholstered in Morris's *Daffodil* chintz.

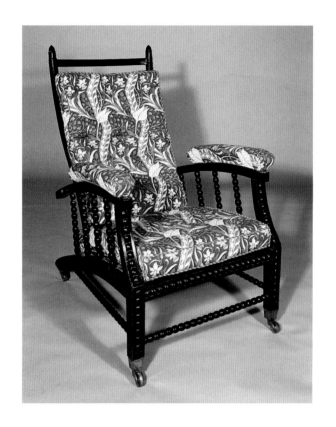

Chrysanthemum Wallpaper

WILLIAM MORRIS, 1876; print design. Victoria & Albert Museum, London.
Although he did not excel at representing the human form, Morris is regarded as a master draftsman. His wallpaper designs are remarkable for their flowing, intertwining patterns.

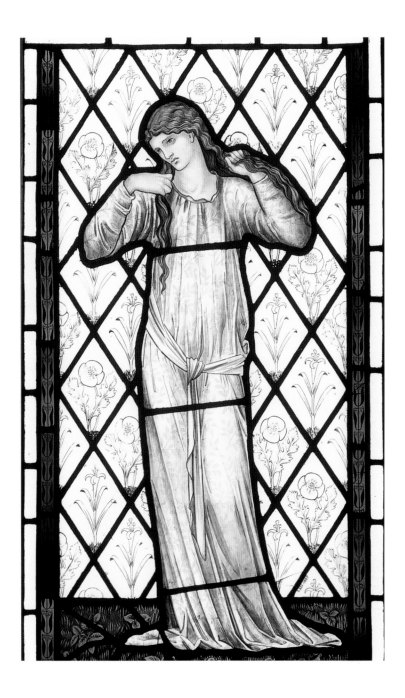

Elaine

EDWARD BURNE-JONES, executed by Morris & Co., c. 1880;

stained glass. Victoria & Albert Museum, London.

Between them, Morris, Webb, and Maddox Brown would design
nearly three hundred stained-glass windows. Burne-Jones, regarded as the most talented in this area, produced at least as
many himself. Predictably, however, stained glass was a profoundly collaborative endeavor.

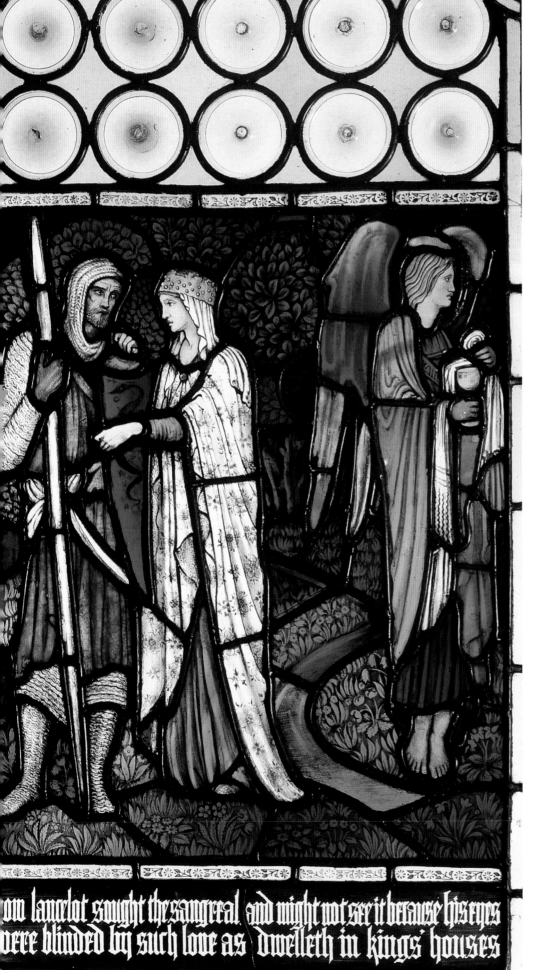

**Lancelot and
the Search for
the Holy Grail**

*EDWARD BURNE-JONES,
c.1880; stained-glass. Victoria
& Albert Museum, London.*
The firm's stained-glass
designs were hardly con-
fined to sacred topics.
Any kind of story-telling
by Morris and Burne-
Jones was bound to in-
volve themes and charac-
ters of Arthurian legend.

ow lancelot sought the sangreal and might not see it because his eyes
were blinded by such love as dwelleth in kings' houses

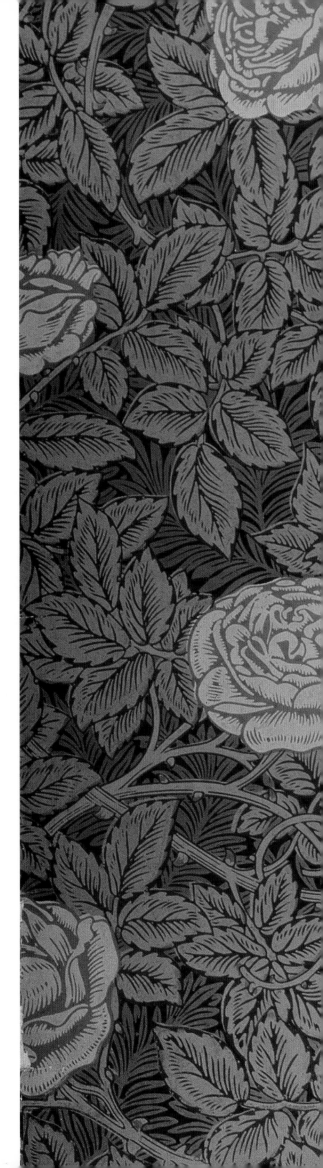

Rose

WILLIAM MORRIS, c. 1880s; print design.
Victoria & Albert Museum, London.
Morris's wallpaper and cotton print
designs are notable for their intricately detailed backgrounds. Rossetti
considered Morris the be the finest
draftsman he had ever known.

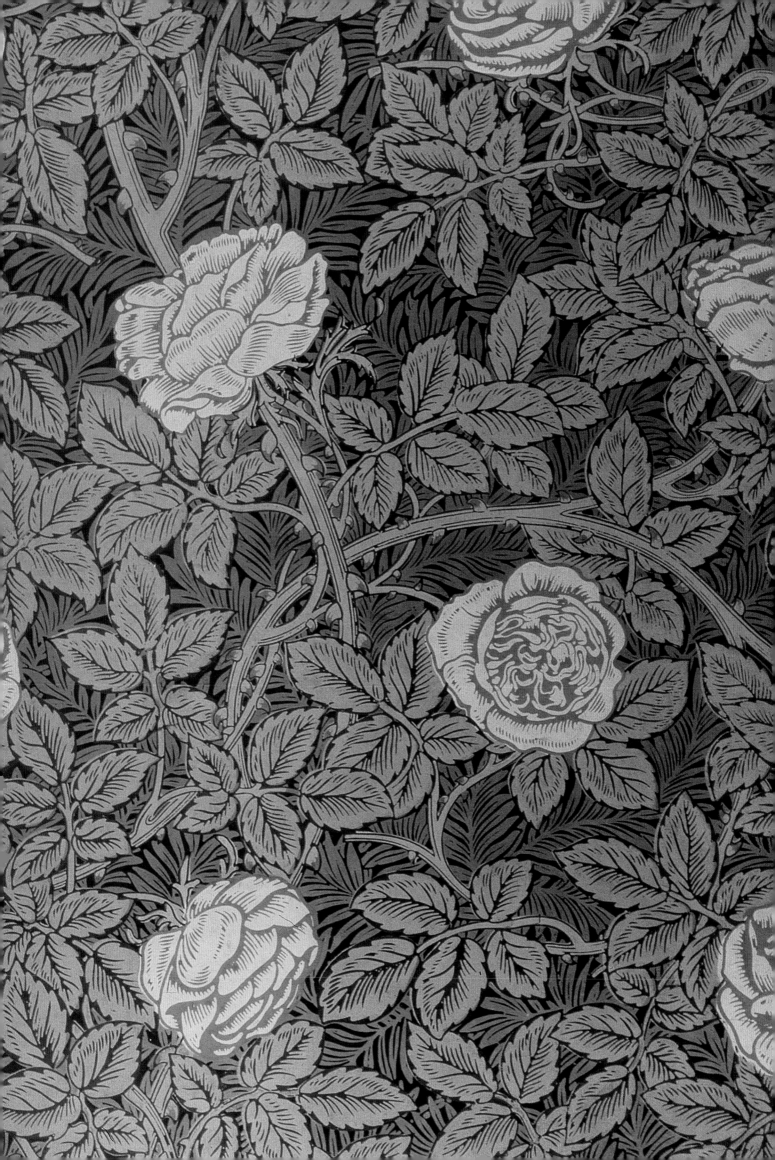

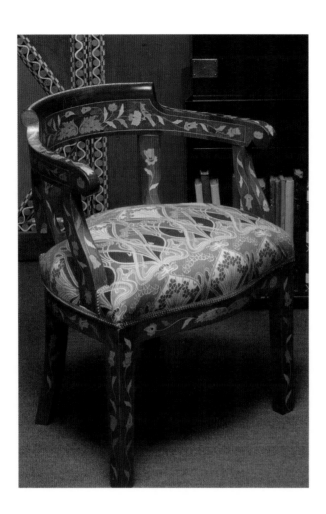

Inlaid chair with William Morris Upholstery

Unknown designer, early twentieth century. Waldbuhl house, Uzwil, Switzerland. The elaborate floral inlays of this chair echo the Morris-designed fabric with which it is upholstered. Morris' textiles continued to be produced well into the twentieth century.

Blue Fruit

WILLIAM MORRIS, 1866; wallpaper design; Victoria & Albert Museum, London. Also known as *Fruit* or *Pomegranate*, *Blue Fruit* is considered to be the most sophisticated of Morris's early wallpaper designs, though still a long way off from the complexity of *Compton*.

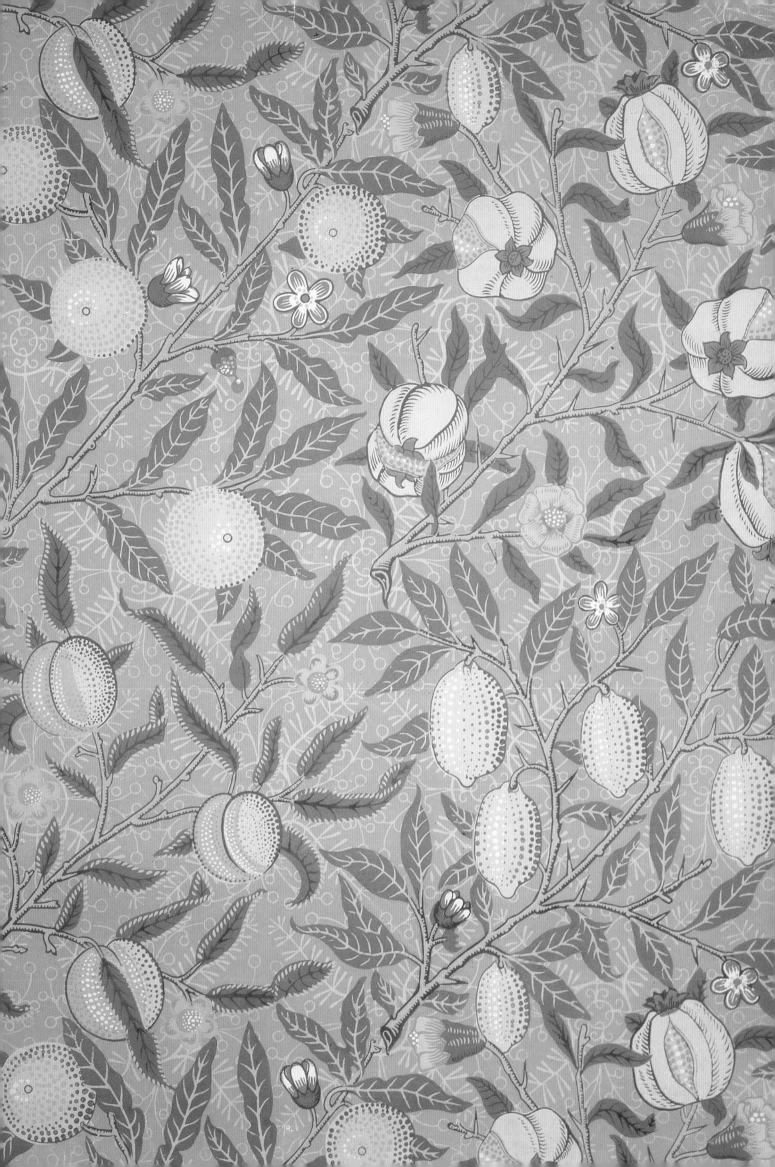

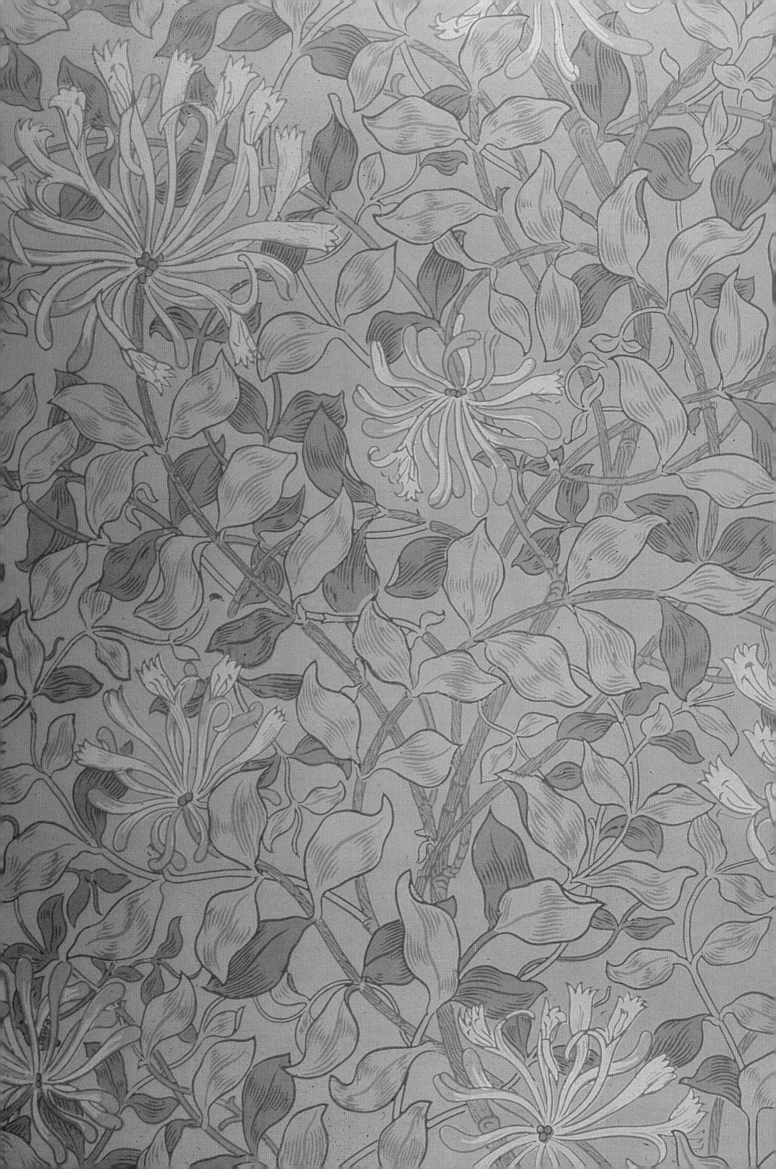

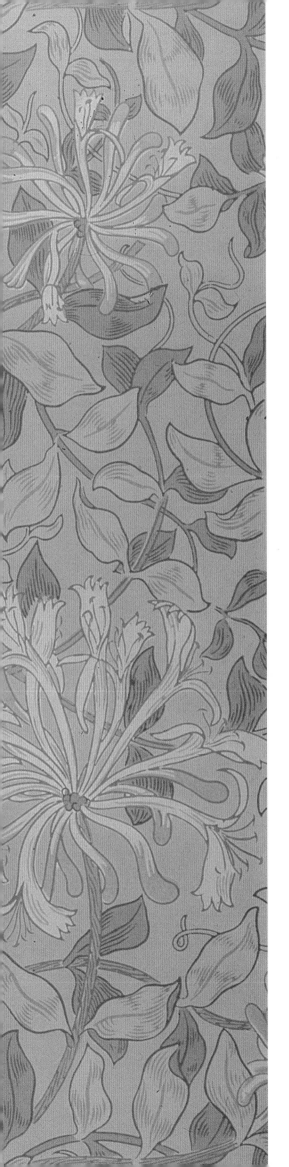

Honeysuckle Wallpaper

WILLIAM MORRIS, n.d.; print design.
Victoria & Albert Museum, London.
Morris used recurrent themes in his
textiles, wallpapers, and tapestries,
often reinterpreting similar patterns
over and over in different media.

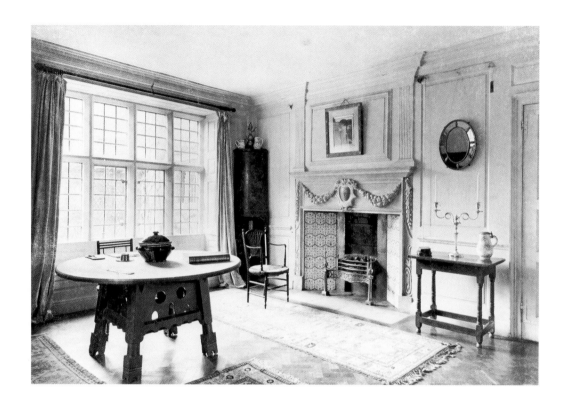

Interior of Morris's Kelmscott Manor home, Oxfordshire.

1871; archival photograph. The Hulton Getty Picture Collection Limited.
At the time, visitors to Kelmscott would have been struck by the
simplicity of furnishings and the expanses of space in Morris's home.
In his lifestyle as in his design, Morris revolted against the Victorian
tendency to clutter rooms with the ornate and the non-functional.

William Morris

*Artist unknown. The Hulton
Getty Picture Collection Limited.*
Throughout his life, Morris was
known for his temper and emotional
volatility. Social theorist Raymond
Williams described Morris's political
rhetoric as "often no more than
a kind of generalized swearing."

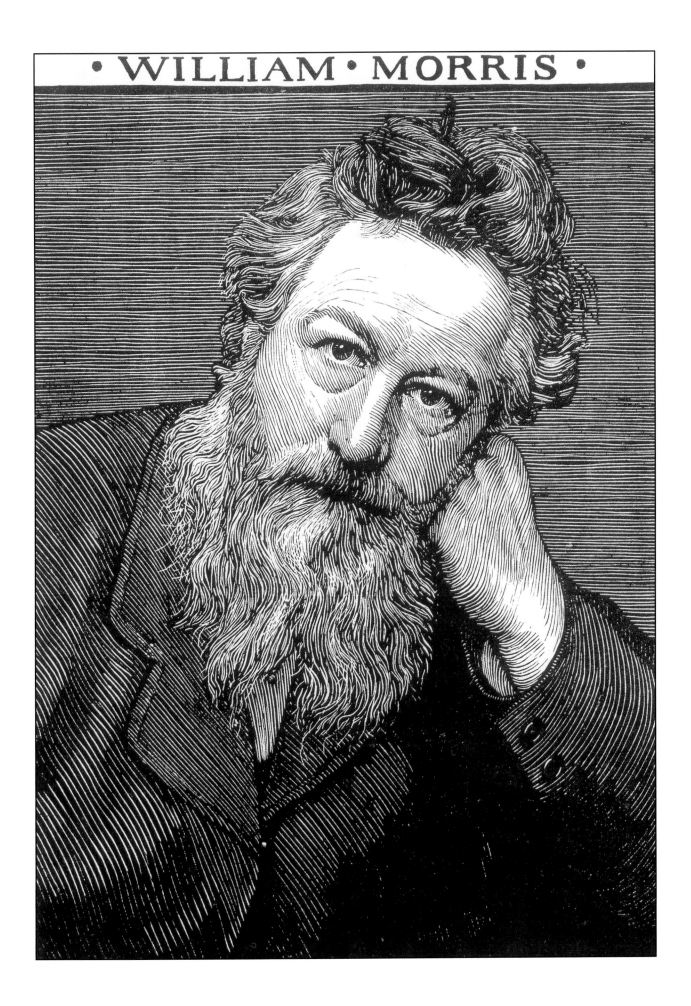

· WILLIAM · MORRIS ·

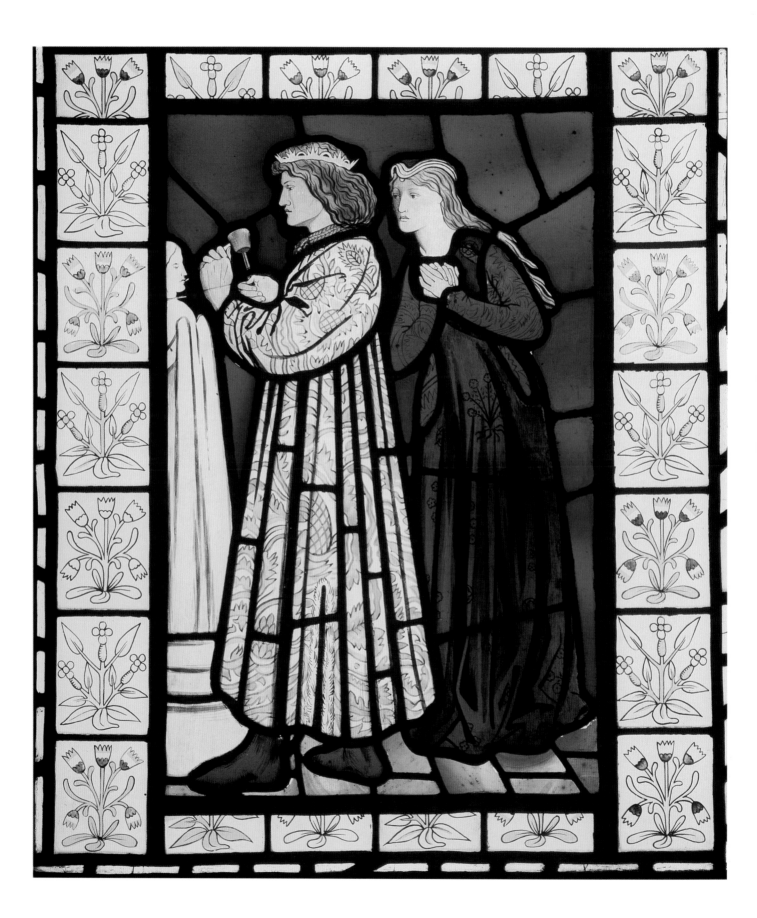

Chapter Three

DOWN TO BUSINESS: MORRIS & CO. REDESIGNS VICTORIAN ENGLAND

The growth of Decorative Arts in this country, owing to the efforts of English Architects, has now reached a point at which it seems desirable that Artists of reputation should devote their time to it. Although no doubt particular instances of success may be cited, still it must be generally felt that attempts of this kind hitherto have been crude and fragmentary. Up to this time, the want of that artistic supervision, which can alone bring about harmony between the various parts of a successful work, has been increased by the necessarily excessive outlay, consequent on taking one individual artist from his pictorial labours.

The Artists whose names appear above hope by association to do away with this difficulty. Having among their number men of varied qualifications, they will be able to undertake any species of decoration, mural or otherwise, from pictures properly so-called, down to the consideration of the smallest work susceptible of art beauty.

. . . and it is believed that good decoration, involving rather the luxury of taste than the luxury of costliness, will be found to be much less expensive than is generally supposed.

—*From the Prospectus of Morris, Marshall, Faulkner & Co.,1861*

In such bold and cocky language did Morris and his partners announce their intentions in April of 1861. According to Rossetti's account, the idea was something of a lark, the result of another all night conversation about medieval guilds and the degraded state of English decorative arts in the industrial era. The perhaps inordinate confidence of the prospectus reflects the grand success of the Red House and, according to Morris's biographer J.W. MacKail, the typically arrogant rhetoric of Rossetti, an artist with a capital A. In truth, Morris was experiencing for the first time some doubts about his financial stability. The Devonshire copper mine shares had dropped rapidly and his annual salary was in danger.

His responsibilities had grown; in 1861 Jane gave birth to a daughter, Jane (called Jenny), and a year later, to another, named May. For the first time in his life, he tasted something like urgency.

The firm, as originally constituted, formed a complimentary balance of artists and more pragmatic businessmen, or so it was hoped. Rossetti, Burne-Jones, Ford Maddox Brown, and Philip Webb brought their artistic reputations to the table. Charles Faulkner was a mathematician, P.P. Marshall a surveyor. Morris, Marshall, and Faulkner were chosen for top billing because it was thought that their names would emphasize the practical and functional intent of the endeavor better than the names of

Sculpture

Morris, Marshall, Faulkner & Co., 1862; From King Rene's Honeymoon *stained-glass series. Victoria & Albert Museum, London.* Stained-glass designs were the most important of the firm's early commissions. In the late 1870s, Morris, who had designed over one hundred windows himself, decided that the firm should no longer produce stained-glass because it contributed to the architectural restoration trend that he opposed.

the well-known artists in their fold. Morris assumed the duties of manager, of which he would make an awful mess, and Faulkner became the firm's accountant. As one would expect, the business affairs of the firm were chaotic in the early years. Morris was simply too obsessed with art to discharge his administrative duties efficiently, and though the firm was always busy and successful in reputation, it was perpetually on the brink of financial ruin due to haphazard management.

Ultimately, each man brought a unique specialization to the firm's projects. Webb designed the lion's share of the furniture, including, ironically, the famed Morris chair. Burne-Jones developed a renowned talent for stained-glass designs, and it was stained-glass with which the firm first established its reputation. Morris, for his part, contributed the best embroideries, wallpapers, and carpets, the intricate and flowing plant designs that would continue to be produced well into the twentieth-century. But it was the synthesis of talents and the over-arching philosophical unity of the firm that provided consistency to their efforts. Their ambitions were great, and, where cost was concerned, unrealistic. In most respects, however, they remained true to their mission, and in so doing, cleared the clutter out of Victorian homes and established a lasting and influential standard for decorative arts.

The Principles of the Firm

Prior to the formation of Morris's firm and the subsequent arts and crafts movement in England, an ornamental clutter and fussiness tended to characterize Victorian interior decor. It was a time of various revivals—Gothic, Italian Renaissance, and others—but no distinct *zeitgeist*. Most critics, Morris among them, attributed the proliferation of bric-a-brac to the middle class's zest for acquisition. Functionalism took a back seat to crude displays of wealth, and most Victorian drawing rooms were, to Morris's taste, not only gaudy but quite uncomfortable as

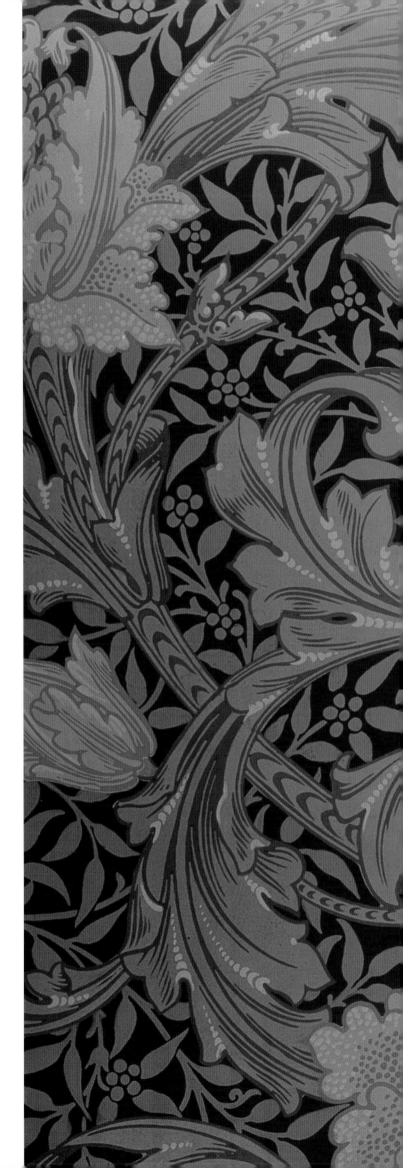

Single Stem

WILLIAM MORRIS, n.d.; print design. Victoria & Albert Museum, London. Morris's dissatisfaction with modern dying techniques led him to explore ancient herbal dying methods and apply them to the firm's prints. He was especially proud of his indigo dyes.

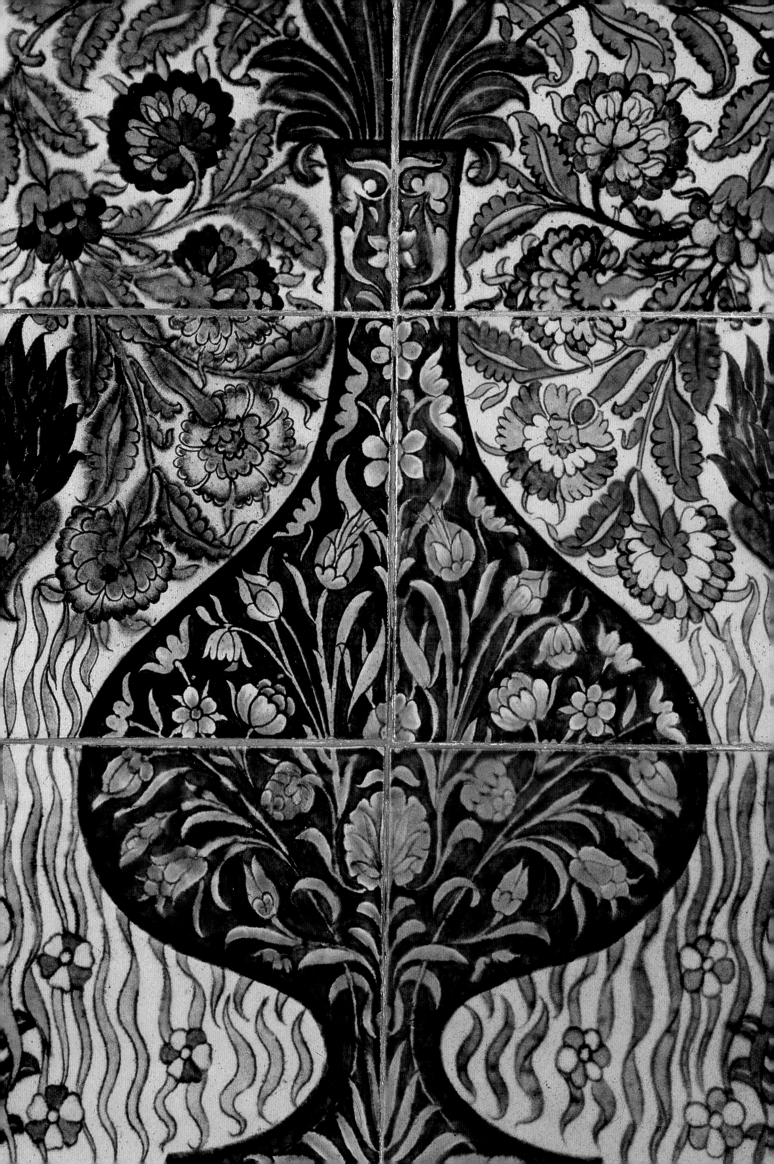

well. New and abundant techniques of mass production fed the popular hunger for novelty and ornament. "Shoddy is king," Morris is reported to have said. Although he might not have recognized it at the time, he and Burne-Jones's "Holy Warfare against the age" was to begin on the battlefields of bedroom and dining room, on the walls and floors of English homes.

A revival of the decorative arts in England was already well under way when Morris established his firm. In 1851, Henry Cole had organized the "Great Exhibition," a display of largely mass-produced furniture and home decorations meant to herald a new era in British practical arts. Even at the time, the young Morris had thought the famous exhibition vulgar. Ten years later, mass-produced decor was the status quo against which the firm revolted. It was Morris's contention, following Ruskin, that labor undertaken with joy and a sense of meaning would yield a superior product. Mechanical, repetitive, and isolated labor, therefore, was much to blame for the bland, spiritless perfection of mass-produced art. Art, Morris was coming to understand, is a reflection of prevailing social conditions. Thus, the conscientious and committed craftsman was, in his own quiet way, a revolutionary. By producing wholesome household art and making it available to people of all circumstances, the firm would be subtly effecting a change in society.

Morris, Marshall, Faulkner & Co. looked to the past not so much for the substance of their work, although a medieval flavor was ever-present, but for the spirit in which the work would be produced and used. They fervently opposed the separation of design and production, a trend initiated during the Renaissance and deeply entrenched in the industrial age. The factory laborer or, worse yet, the machine, took no part in the larger artistic conception and thus could hardly be expected to imbue his/its work with sensitivity and a sense of pride. Similarly, the designer with clean hands would be less likely to bring about that desired "harmony between the various parts" of a work

of art. Morris's hands, it is worth noting, were famously blue, a result of his extensive experimentation with dyes. The members of the firm offered themselves, then, as modern incarnations of the medieval craftsman, he who gained fluency in production and execution as well as the techniques of design. In this regard, Morris was exemplary. He studied and mastered the minutiae of dyeing, weaving, embroidering, etc., before commencing with designs.

Extending this same time-consuming luxury to all workers at the firm proved to be a more difficult (and finally impossible) proposition. While there was a business to be run, there would always be tedium and repetition. As many have pointed out, Morris was hardly above contracting out menial jobs to other firms where the gratification of workers was not a top priority, and, in cases where artistic quality would not be seriously compromised, using machines. Much of the firm's work was done on commission for particular houses, thus mass reproduction was not required and the medieval ideal could be honored. However, in the case of commercially marketed wallpapers, Morris soon realized the futility of doing it all in his own shop.

It bothered him to no end that his workers were still caught in the trap of a "profit-grinding society" and that he could do little to liberate them. In addition, many of the less creative but necessary jobs—pattern copying and tile painting, for example—were handled by women, by Jane Morris and by Charles Faulkner's two sisters. This dissonance between philosophy and practice was not lost on Morris. Paradoxes like these ultimately fired his interest in the political world, especially regarding the political implications of art. When Morris finally came to feel that great art was simply not possible under the current social conditions, he shifted his attention almost entirely to the political arena. Still, the efforts of the firm during its peak years were a noble attempt, an ambitious demonstration of how the pleasures of art can enrich everyday living.

Floral Tiles

WILLIAM MORRIS, n.d.;
painted ceramic tiles.
Victoria & Albert
Museum, London.
While Morris was heavily involved in almost every phase of production on his famous textiles and wallpapers, duties such as painting tiles were often left to women, including Jane Morris, and Charles Faulkner's sisters.

The Products of the Firm: Stained Glass

The firm's breakthrough came at the International Exhibition at the South Kensington Museum (now the Victoria and Albert) in 1862, where *The Parable of the Vineyard*, seven stained-glass panels by Rossetti, attracted enough attention to arouse suspicion in other exhibitors; perhaps, some thought, the panels were actual medieval artifacts touched up and refurbished for the occasion. The success at South Kensington led to the most significant of the firm's early commissions. Well-known church architect G.F. Bodley hired the firm to produce windows for several new churches, including Jesus College Chapel and All Saint's Church in Cambridge, and Selsley in Gloucestershire. There could not have been a more propitious beginning. As part of the general Gothic revival, churches were springing up all over England. Although the artists of the firm were more interested in secular design, they had no qualms about riding that trend to greater recognition and more commissions. In all, the firm's stained-glass work graces over six hundred churches and museums in several countries.

Between them, Morris, Webb, and Maddox Brown would design nearly three hundred stained-glass windows. Burne-Jones, regarded as the most talented in this area, produced at least as many himself. Predictably, however, the stained-glass was a profoundly collaborative

The Gold of Love and Alcestis

Morris, Marshall, Faulkner & Co., 1864; stained glass window. Victoria & Albert Museum, London. Although Rossetti designed the firm's most early important stained-glass and Burne-Jones was the most prolific in this department, Morris contributed significantly by working with dyes and color patterns. The firm's stained-glass was considered to be the finest English specimens since the Middle Ages.

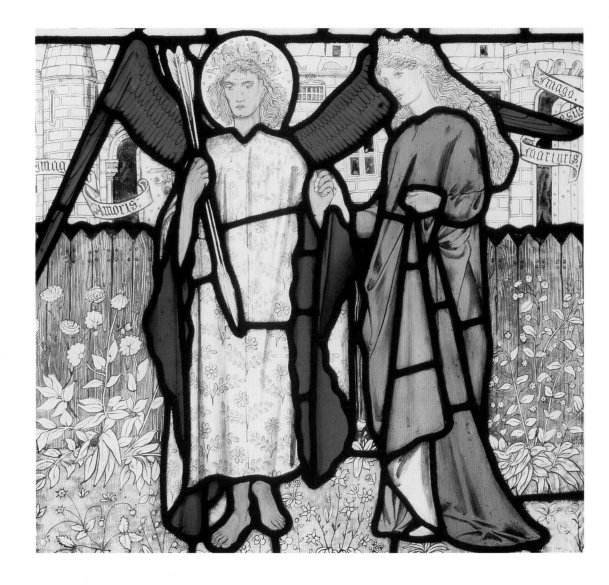

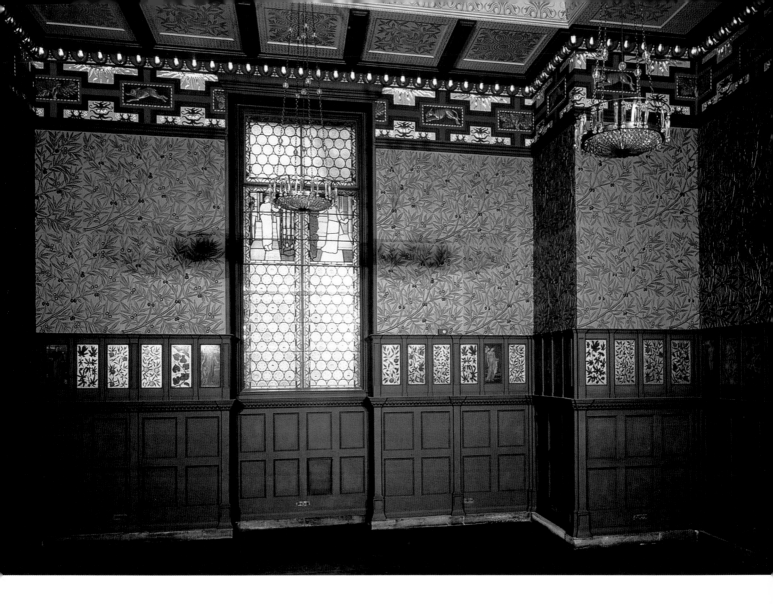

endeavor. Morris takes credit for the striking and luminous color schemes. He developed an original yellow dye that was remarkably flexible in covering a wide tonal range. A relative unknown, George Campfield, foreman at the firm's Red Lion Square works, was an exquisite and experienced glass painter and no doubt shared his expertise with the artists who would reap the credit for the windows.

It is somewhat ironic that the firm, a generally agnostic or nominally Christian lot, should begin their collective career in ecclesiastical settings. This was hardly the overture to the common people that their prospectus had promised. Later, Morris would regret the quantity of stained-glass produced by the firm for a different reason; he had, against his better instincts, participated in the trend of Gothic revival, a phenomenon to which he was, or would become, philosophically opposed. What's more, he had built his business reputation upon it. Such perilous paradoxes were all in a day's work for Morris.

Perhaps Morris expressed his disdain for the capitalist nature of the enterprise by neglecting finances altogether. Had the firm charged the going rate for stained-glass, it could have made a tidy fortune. Certainly, its clients in this market—churches and museums—were wealthy, hardly the clientele Morris had in mind when he promised to make beautiful things available to ordinary people. But early on, Morris and his colleagues developed the habit of under-charging and failing to maintain an adequate profit margin. George Warrington Taylor, who became the firm's business manager after Faulkner returned to Oxford in the late 1860s, continually prodded the group to pay more attention to costing and profit. He was particularly irked by the stained-glass commissions because the firm had failed to charge separately for designs and actual windows, thus cheating themselves out of considerable revenue. Before his early death in 1870, Taylor may have rescued the firm from ruin, but he could do little to foster greater financial awareness in the artists. With their reputation built solidly on stained-glass work, they turned their attention, their war against the prevailing tastes of the day, to the domestic front.

The Green Dining Room, South Kensington

Morris, Marshall, Faulkner & Co., 1867. Victoria & Albert Museum, London. Designed by Webb but involving all the members of the firm, the Green Dining Room at South Kensington was among the firm's most important early commissions. It enabled them to display in a coherent fashion the range of items they produced.

67

Furniture

Chairs should be comfortable; tables and cabinets should be well-built, lasting, and versatile; style and ornament should never compromise utility; those articles that are basic to the enjoyment of life should accommodate, and not contort, the human body. These homely and obvious values may have been lost amidst the Victorian revival craze.

If so, the furniture designs of Morris, Marshall, Faulkner, and Co. played a key part in a culture's rediscovery of the elegance of simplicity. The firm's furniture style, especially as expressed in its many and various chairs, was an anti-style, a plain and sturdy character that must have shocked Victorian eyes with its unadorned directness.

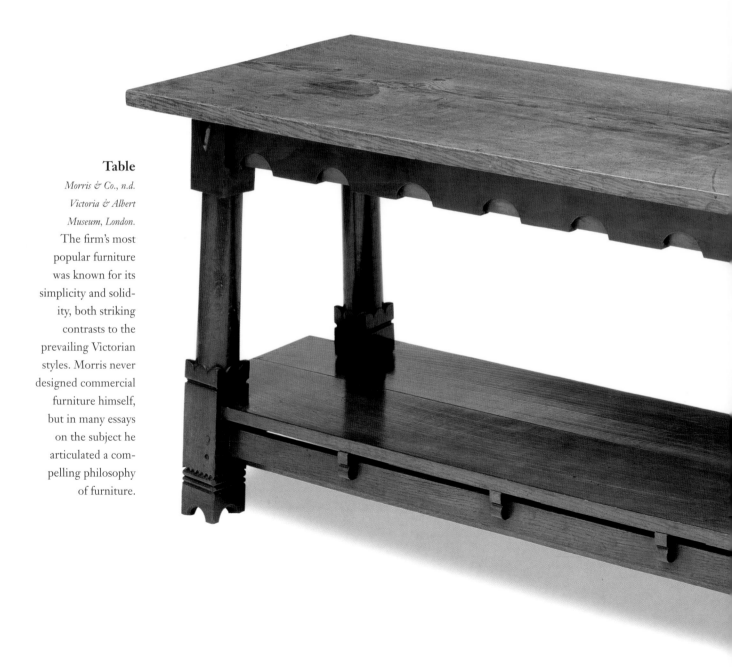

Table

Morris & Co., n.d.
Victoria & Albert
Museum, London.
The firm's most popular furniture was known for its simplicity and solidity, both striking contrasts to the prevailing Victorian styles. Morris never designed commercial furniture himself, but in many essays on the subject he articulated a compelling philosophy of furniture.

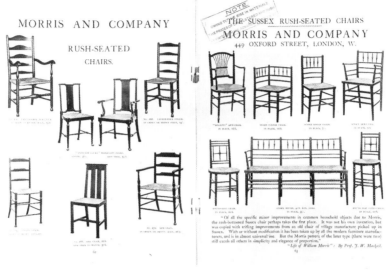

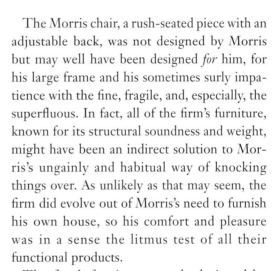

Morris & Co. Catalogue

c. 1911. William Morris Gallery London.

The sussex rush-seated chairs were the firm's least expensive and most popular items of furniture. For this reason, Morris regarded them as one of his most important contributions to English decor.

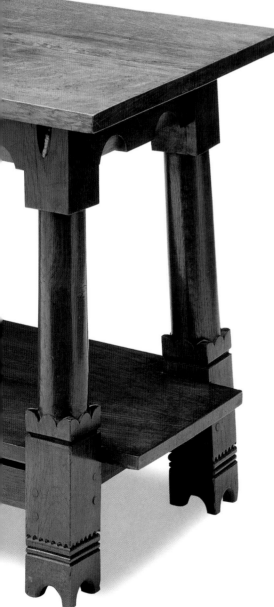

The Morris chair, a rush-seated piece with an adjustable back, was not designed by Morris but may well have been designed *for* him, for his large frame and his sometimes surly impatience with the fine, fragile, and, especially, the superfluous. In fact, all of the firm's furniture, known for its structural soundness and weight, might have been an indirect solution to Morris's ungainly and habitual way of knocking things over. As unlikely as that may seem, the firm did evolve out of Morris's need to furnish his own house, so his comfort and pleasure was in a sense the litmus test of all their functional products.

The firm's furniture, mostly designed by Philip Webb, quickly became its most popular and best-selling product. Its austerity of design and simple solidity of construction were a direct challenge to the popular Empire and Rococo furniture styles of the moment, styles characterized by brass, marble, and leather embellishment. The firm produced two kinds of furniture: the practical and inexpensive kind, like the Morris chair, and a more ornate and decorative kind with hand-painted panels and fine carving which Morris referred to as "state" furniture. The state furniture—cabinets, sideboards, desks, beds, and even a piano designed

Sideboard

Morris & Co, n.d.. Victoria &
Albert Museum, London.
The firm's pieces of furniture
were generally collaborative
endeavors, especially the more
ornate and expensive ones, such
as this sideboard. Philip Webb
designed most of the pieces, but
panels might be painted by Rossetti, de Morgan, or Burne-Jones.

by Webb—sold well, but it was in the
simple and affordable variety in which
the firm came closest to realizing its goal
of furnishing the homes of ordinary
people, not just the well-to-do.

Although Morris designed very little
furniture himself, he regarded furniture
as the firm's most significant product.
In the end, precious little of his work was
within the financial reach of the working classes, and furniture, especially the

Sussex chairs, was the most notable
exception. Other products—stained-
glass, embroideries, earthenware—
received more critical acclaim. Morris's
wallpapers would prove to be more
lasting. The furniture, however, best
succeeded at bridging the abyss between
serious art and everyday life. It was a
social as well as an artistic success, at
the time the fullest realization of the
firm's two-fold mission.

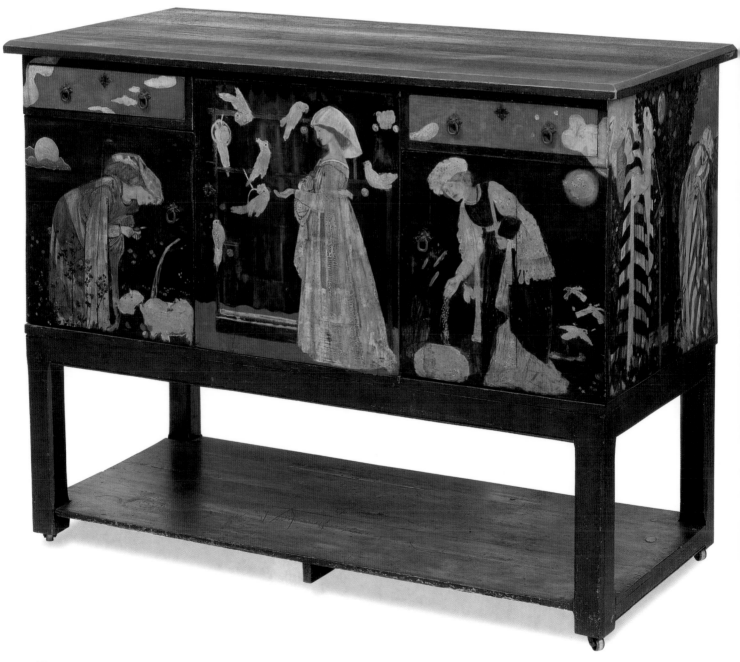

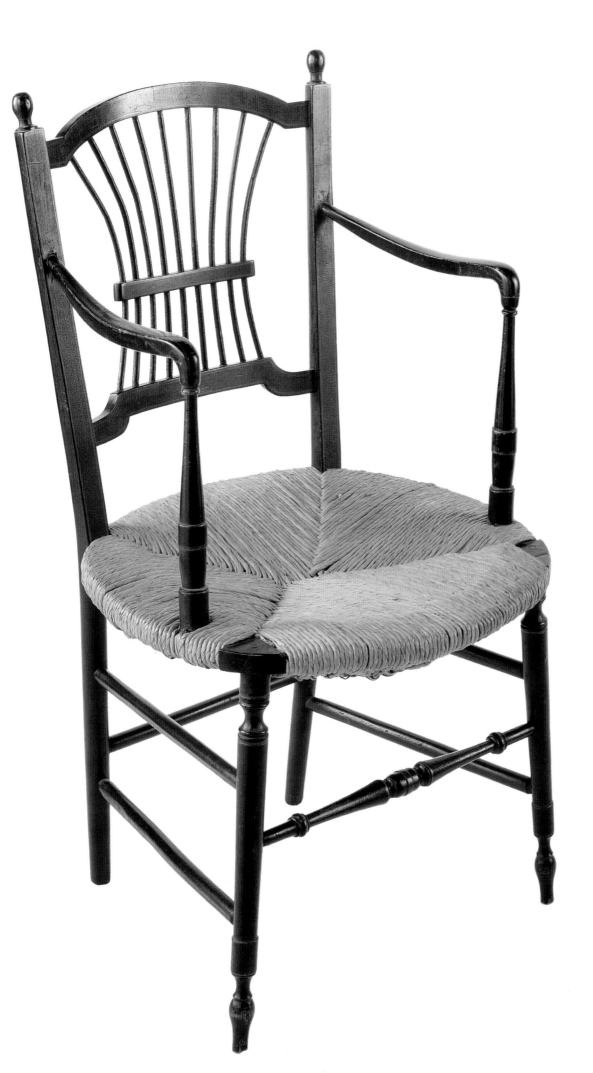

FOLLOWING PAGE:
Printed linoleum floor cover
Designed by WILLIAM MORRIS, 1875; printed linoleum. Victoria & Albert Museum, London.
This linoleum was Morris's first floor cover design of any kind, and his first and only linoleum. His firm lacked the facilities to produce linoleum and he generally disapproved of machine-made decorations. The firm would become well known for its carpets.

Rossetti Armchair
Designer unknown, c. 1860s. Victoria & Albert Museum, London.
This lyre-back chair was a variation on the sussex style that defined the firm's more affordable furniture. Chairs like this sold for as little as ten or fifteen shillings and continued to be produced in the twentieth century.

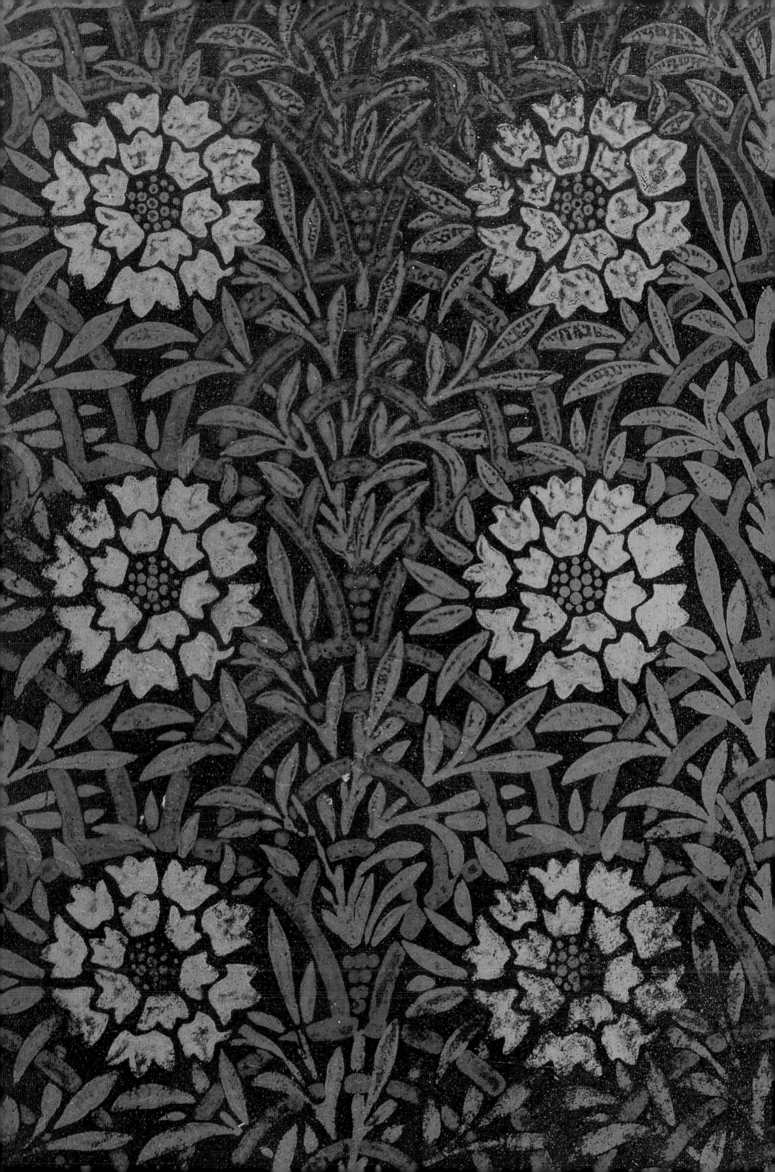

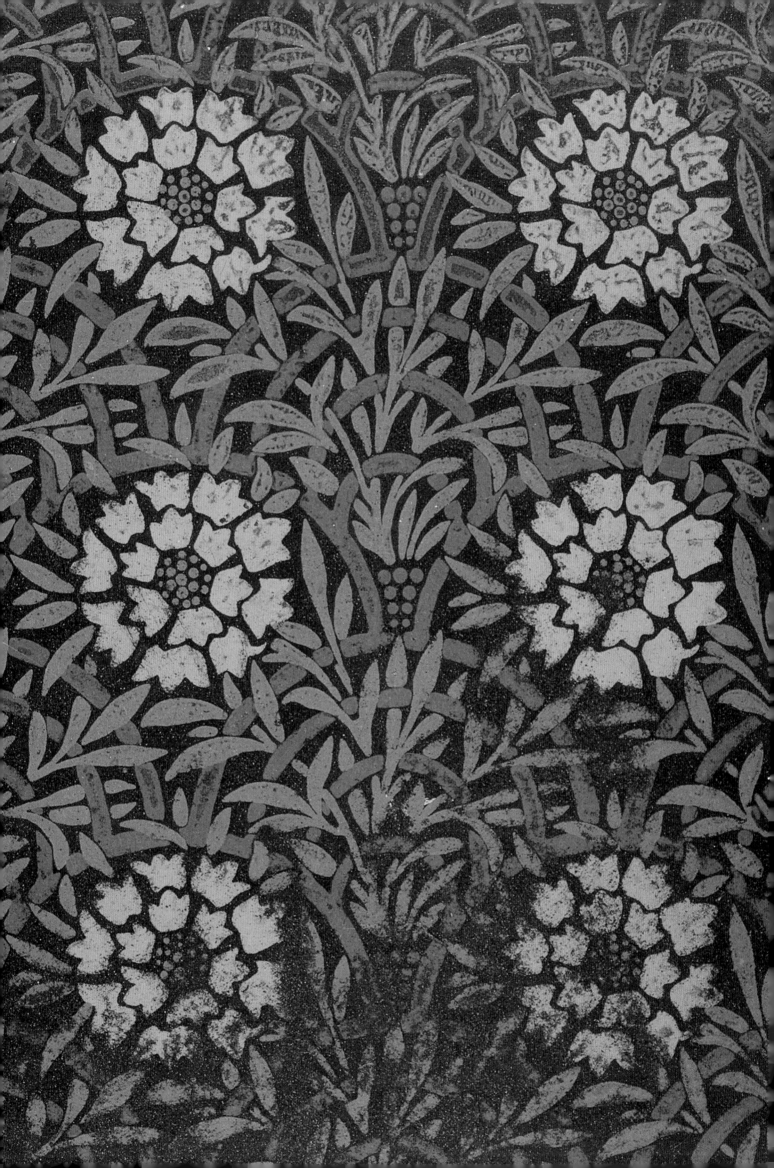

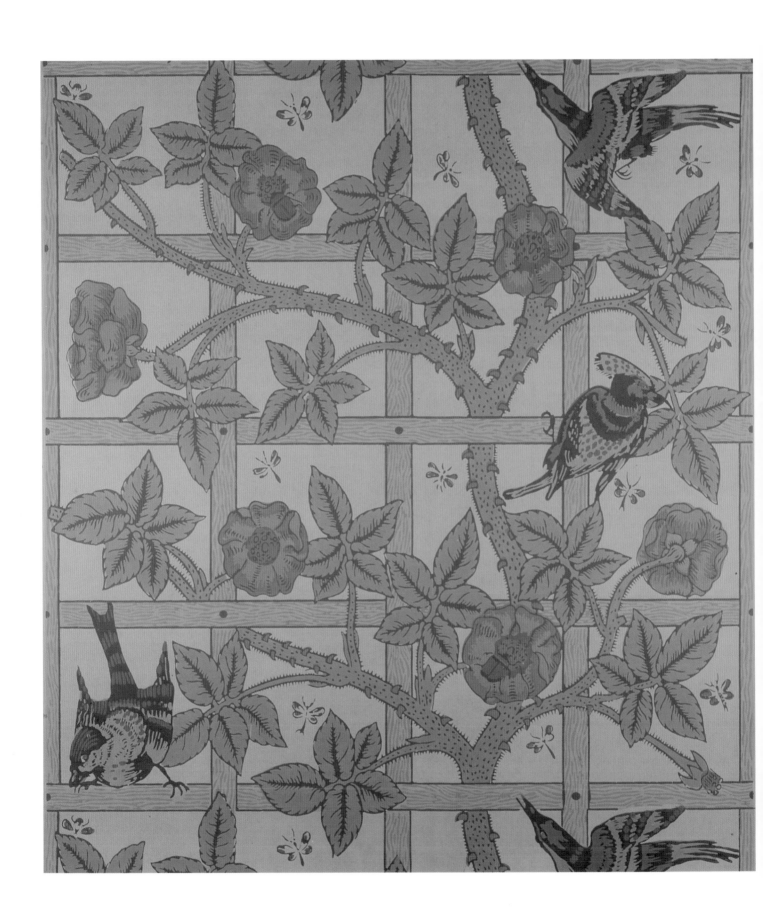

Textiles

Carpets, tapestries, wallpapers, chintzes— William Morris's abundant textile designs captured the natural imagery embedded in his imagination, the complex and interdependent patterns that he had absorbed as a boy roaming through Epping Forest. Textiles would become his specialty, the area in which he excelled above all others, and of all the firm's designs and products, Morris's wallpapers are the only ones still commercially available today. Their lasting popularity is due to a combination of qualities: the textures are dense and rich, but the individual forms—flowers, thickets, birds—remain distinct and flowing. Detail worthy of close study abounds but always in the service of a cumulative, consistent effect, a harmonious synthesis of color and form.

As with so much of the firm's work, Morris's interest in textiles dates back to the early days of the Red House and stems from his reluctance to furnish his own house with inferior mass-produced items. Over a period of many years, he put in endless hours learning the fine points of weaving and embroidering, escaping the boredom of repetition by composing poetry in his head. The textile media allowed Morris's strongest talents to shine—his draftsmanship, his facility with colors, his graceful lines, and his deep feel for the individual forms and symbiotic relationships of nature. Importantly, textiles also allowed him to avoid that with which he was least comfortable, the human form. When human figures were required in a tapestry, Morris's sketches had conspicuous body-shaped blank spaces to be filled in by Burne-Jones.

Morris considered embroidery and weaving to be the highest of the decorative arts, the ones most closely aligned with painting and sculpture. Since most of his carpets and hangings were commissioned by wealthy individuals, there was no need for reproduction and plenty

Morris & Co. Workshops at Merton Abbey
Twentieth century; archival photograph. William Morris Gallery, London.
The establishment of the firm's Merton Abbey works allowed Morris to contract out fewer jobs and supervise the work himself. Pictured here are the jacquard looms that Morris himself had mastered in the 1870s.

Trellis Wallpaper
William Morris, 1864; print design. Victoria & Albert Museum, London.
Inspired by the rose trellises at the Red House, *Trellis* was Morris's first wall paper design. When Morris wanted birds in a design, he would usually call upon the talents of Philip Webb. The architect and furniture specialist also had a way with birds.

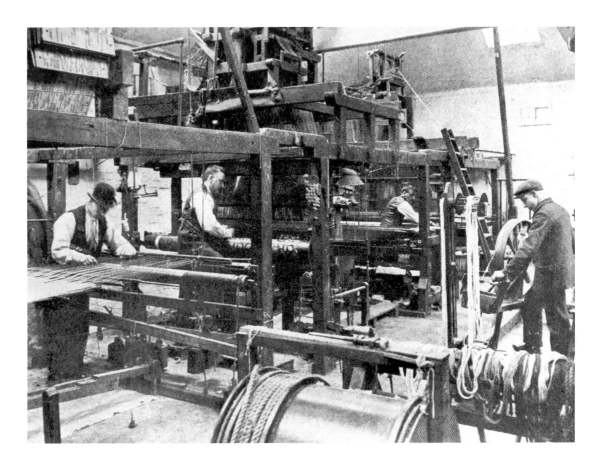

Lily Carpet

*WILLIAM MORRIS,
1877. Victoria & Albert
Museum, London.*
Morris's Kiddermin-
ster carpets, carpets
woven of two or
three different fabrics,
were often imitated
and extremely popular
in the United States.
As with so many of
the firm's products,
Morris mastered
the weaving tech-
nique himself before
turning those duties
over to craftsmen he
himself had trained.

of room for idiosyncrasy and originality. His popular wallpaper, however, required reproduction to meet growing public demand, and for this Morris usually turned to Messrs Jeffrey & Company. With the artist frequently on hand to supervise the cuttings and the colorings, the Islington firm hand-printed his designs using carved wood blocks. A comparison of the first of his forty-one wallpapers, "The Trellis" from 1862 with his last, "Compton" from 1896, the year of his death, reveals an appreciable artistic growth, a development which moved away from the stiff and stylized and toward a remarkable sense of living movement.

In the late 1870s, textiles outstripped furniture and stained-glass as the firm's most popular products. In the process of making chintzes, carpets, and tapestries, the conflict between artistic integrity and commercial necessity would once again come to a head, this time over the issue of dyes. Dyes derived from coal tar, yet another industrial innovation, had generally replaced those obtained from vegetables. But Morris's discriminating taste found the modern dyes lacking in subtlety. He sought the assistance of Thomas Wardle, a noted authority on dyes and silk. From then on, Wardle handled the printing of Morris's chintzes. More importantly, Wardle encouraged Morris to experiment for himself and thus sent him on a journey in search of poplar, osier twigs, and indigo. Legend has Morris scouring Paris for the ancient herbs he needed to test his color combinations.

During these very productive years, Morris also attacked weaving with a vengeance, teaching himself how to weave tapestries with the help of an eighteenth-century French manual and an old loom that, in times of transition, he would set up in his bedroom. The loom would accompany him to his public lectures on the "lesser arts," and for long stretches he would weave with his back to the audience, talking all the while. For Morris, it was enough to learn the basic techniques of a craft and then turn the duties over to qualified workers. In only one instance, the "Cabbage and Vine" tapestry, did Morris complete a project from beginning to end. In this fashion, he saved the bulk of his time for design. Handiwork, however, remained his passion. While he acknowledged and discharged his duties as a businessman with growing efficiency, and while his poetry and not his designs became the chief source of his renown, William Morris still preferred nothing to a day spent lost in a project, hour upon hour spent translating his imagination into image.

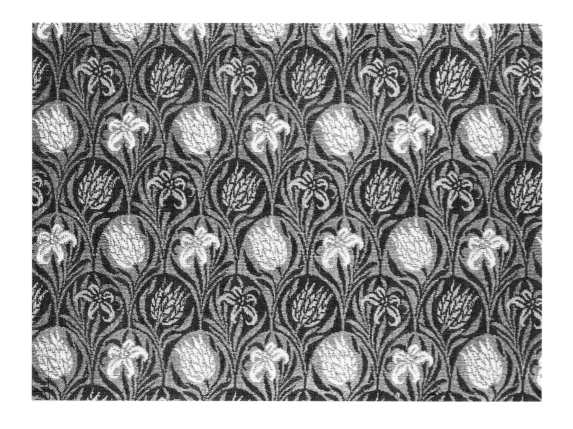

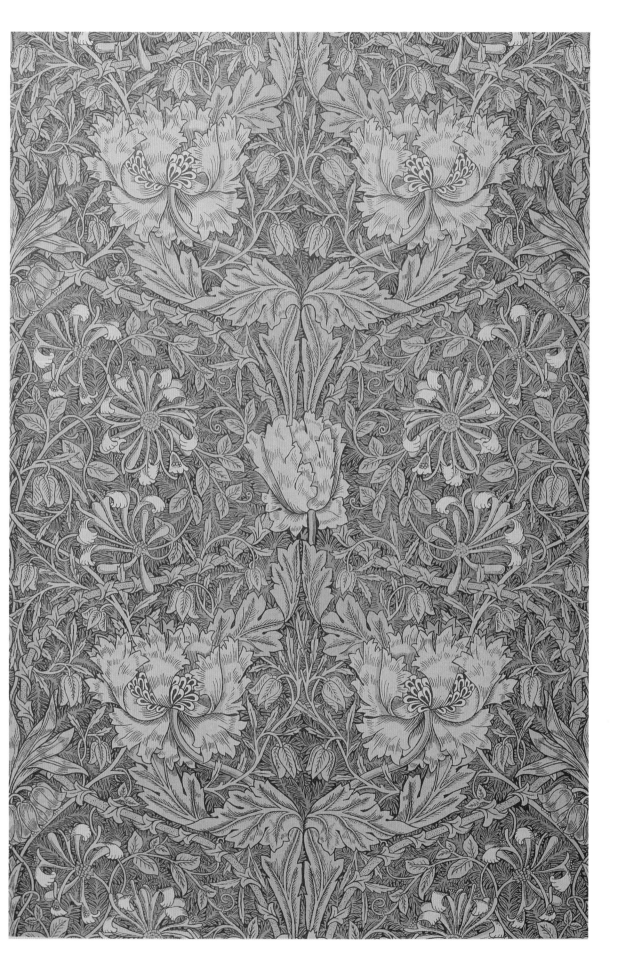

Honeysuckle

*WILLIAM MORRIS,
1876; textile design.
Victoria & Albert
Museum, London.*
This textile design
by Morris was re-
peated in a number
of media, printed
onto linen, cotton,
silk, and velveteen.
It was one of the
first designs by
Morris & Co.
to be printed by
Thomas Wardle.

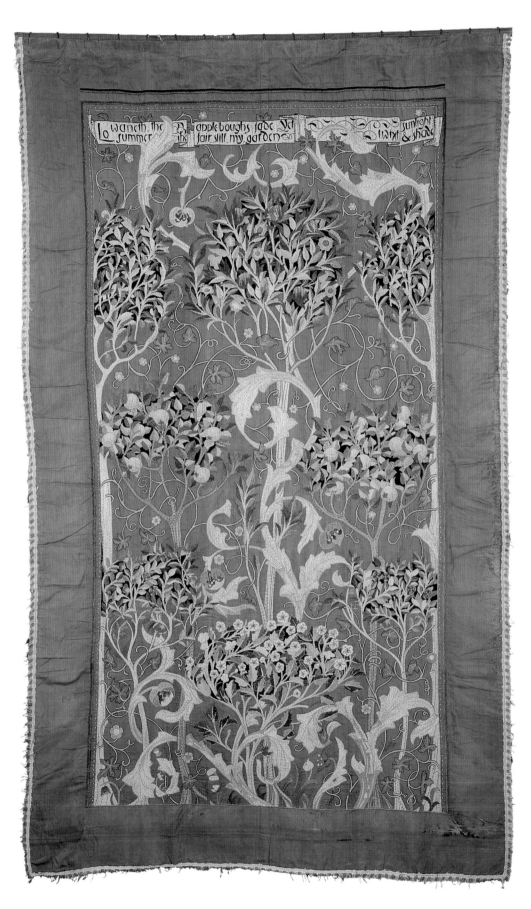

Orchard Portiere

WILLIAM MORRIS, c. 1880s; textile. Victoria & Albert Museum, London. The portiere, a curtain that hangs over a doorway, was an important feature of Victorian homes; it served the dual purpose of decoration and insulation.

Anemone

WILLIAM MORRIS, 1876; textile design. Victoria & Albert Museum, London. Anemone, among the most popular of the firm's repeated patterns, was produced in silk and wool fabric and silk damask. It was one of the first designs produced on a powered loom.

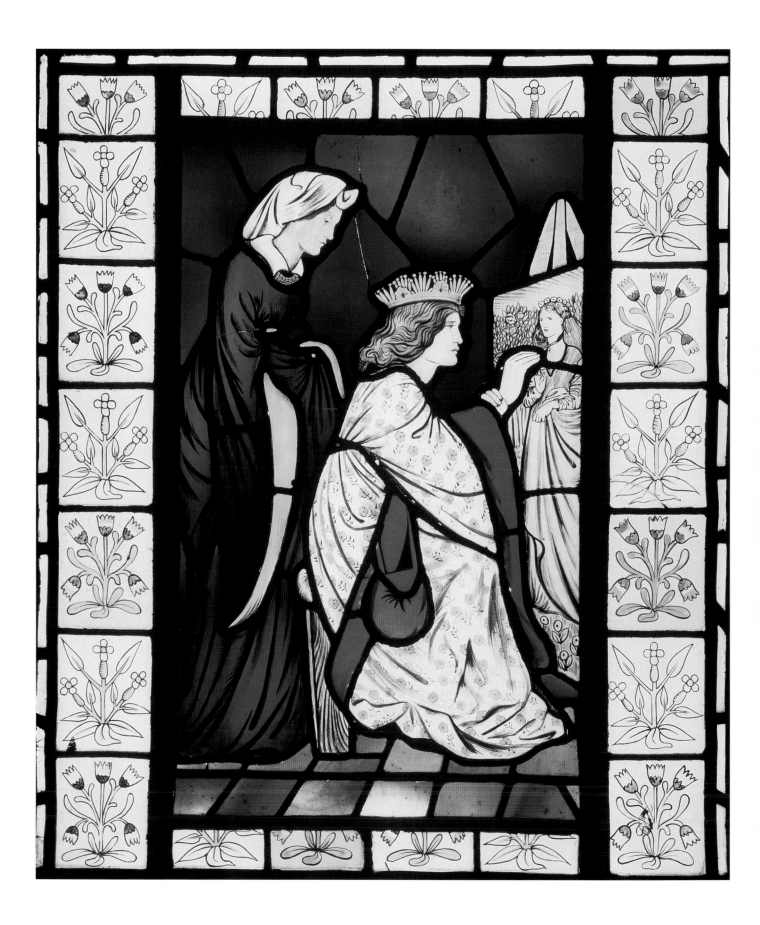

Successes and Failures:
Morris Evaluates the Firm

After many near-disasters and the constant exasperation of his more financially-conscious partners and advisors, Morris finally developed a shrewder business sense. Events in the fourth decade of his life had toughened him, from domestic discontent to his growing fascination with the rugged culture and literary tradition of Iceland. In 1875, he restructured the firm, a move that amounted to the ousting of the less productive partners, notably Maddox Brown and Rossetti. Maddox Brown had devoted most of his time to painting, and Rossetti, for whom Morris had developed a deep and unspoken resentment, had suffered grave physical and mental deterioration due in part to laudanum addiction. Morris and his two dearest friends, Burne-Jones and Webb, remained the firm's principal designers. To reflect the actual hierarchy and chain of command that had presided for years, the firm was renamed Morris & Co.

Outwardly, the enterprise had been an unqualified success. Morris and his partners made a decent living, a fact all the sweeter because they could have been infinitely wealthier if they availed themselves of modern production techniques. Insofar as it was possible, they had maintained artistic integrity and managed a successful and reasonably prosperous business. They had exerted a profound and lasting influence over a remarkably wide area. The Red House modeled a new and bracing philosophy of architectural simplicity that would be cited as an important precursor of the Bauhaus and other twentieth-century schools of design. Their stained-glass and other ecclesiastical work re-introduced medieval values without resorting to mimicry. Their vast array of household products challenged and ultimately changed the tastes of the consuming public and set the stage for the arts and crafts movement of the late-nineteenth and early-twentieth centuries.

Above all, the firm achieved a cumulative impact, one not attributable to any specific product or production technique. They had, through persistent emphasis on functionality and simple quality, opened up living spaces, cleared away the irrelevant and ostentatious, and reinvigorated the decorative arts as a source of necessary daily pleasure and satisfaction. If Morris's influence as a designer and champion of functional art can be reduced to a single sentence, it would be his own famous dictum from the essay "The Beauty of Life": "Have nothing in your houses which you do not know to be useful or believe to be beautiful." The distinction here between "know" and

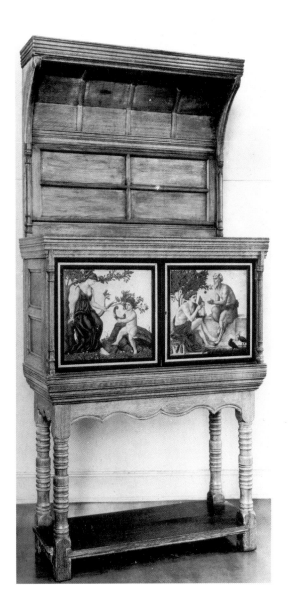

Oak cabinet

Designed by Philip Webb with painted tiles by William de Morgan, n.d.. William Morris Gallery, London. Since the days when Rossetti's paintings adorned the settle that Morris designed for Red Lion Square, the firm's more expensive and ornate furniture was a collaborative enterprise. The firm attempted to achieve a balance of function and beauty.

Painting

Morris, Marshall, Faulkner & Co., 1862; from King Rene's Honeymoon *stained-glass series. Victoria & Albert Museum, London.* Stained-glass panels such as this are a common feature of many British churches, including those designed by G. F. Bodley, a prominent architect and the firm's most important client in the early years.

William Morris

1877; archival photograph.
The Hulton Getty Picture
Collection Limited.
In the late 1870s,
Morris was a man
in between two
careers. The firm
was finally on stable
financial ground,
but Morris's interest
in political and
social issues was
beginning to domi-
nate his attention.

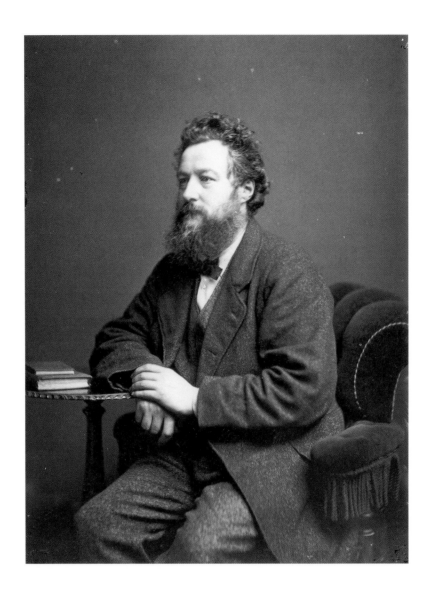

Compton

WILLIAM MORRIS, 1896;
print design. Victoria &
Albert Museum, London.
Produced as both a
chintz and a wall-
paper, *Compton* was one
of William Morris's
last and greatest de-
signs. By the time he
finished *Compton*,
J. H. Dearle and May
Morris were designing
most of the firm's wall-
papers and chintzes.

"believe" is significant and often overlooked. Standards of beauty are highly subjective, in constant flux, and often tainted by motives beyond the purely aesthetic. Utility, for Morris, provided a much more solid standard and ideal, a standard immune to changing fashions and fickle tastes. In Morris's view, useful is beautiful.

However, in Morris's view, the firm had not been an unqualified success. He felt he had failed in the most ambitious and difficult of the firm's missions: to deliver quality and affordable art to all people, and in so doing

to unite all classes of society in an apprecia-tion of beauty. He be-lieved that art had the power to reform not just the appearance but the very structure of society. But by the late 1870s, the firm's hey-day, Morris thought he had done little more than redesign the inte-riors of the wealthy, the Bedford Park minority for whom art and fine objects were signifiers of superiority. Morris loathed the values of the burgeoning middle class and any claim to cultural elitism based on wealth but found that he could not avoid playing into that system, not without making unthinkable sacrifices.

Caught in a self-set trap of hypocrisy, Morris became in-creasingly disillusioned with his work and became convinced that his was an ill society, afflicted with the diseases of greed and inequality. The poverty and abjec-tion of the urban masses troubled him acutely, as did his own privilege. In the last two decades of his life, Morris would make a bold, and not entirely successful, attempt to honor his con-science over his pleasure and direct his ener-gies toward the advancement of the socialist cause. Socialism, he came to believe, was the only way to create a healthy society in which healthy art could flourish and enrich the common wealth.

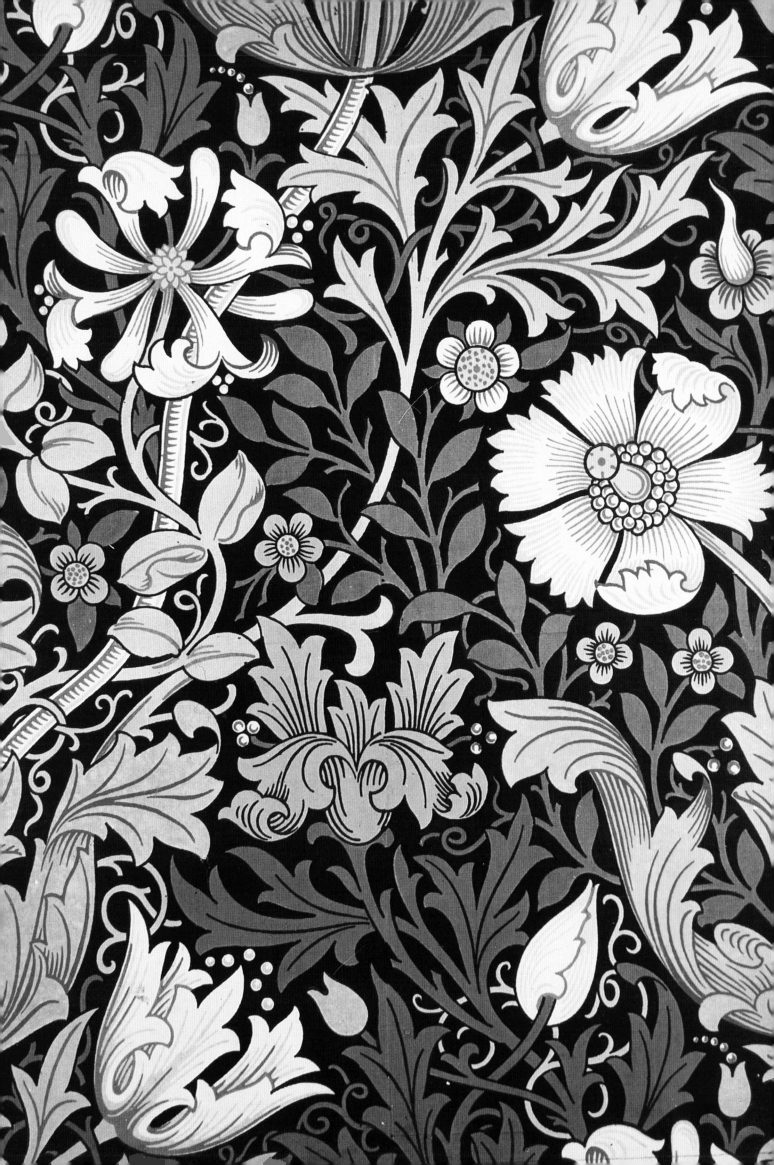

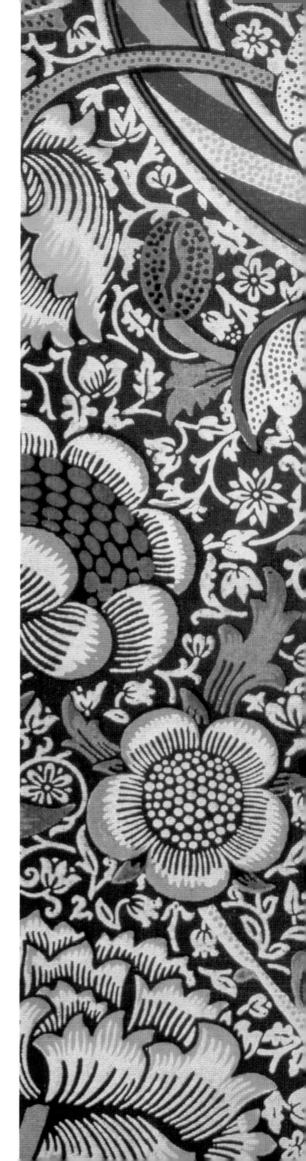

Wandle

detail; WILLIAM MORRIS, c. 1880s; printed
cotton. Victoria & Albert Museum, London.
Of all the media in which Morris
worked, it was in textile design
that his talents—his draftsmanship,
his facility with colors, his graceful lines, and his deep feel for the
individual forms and symbiotic relationships of nature—really shone.

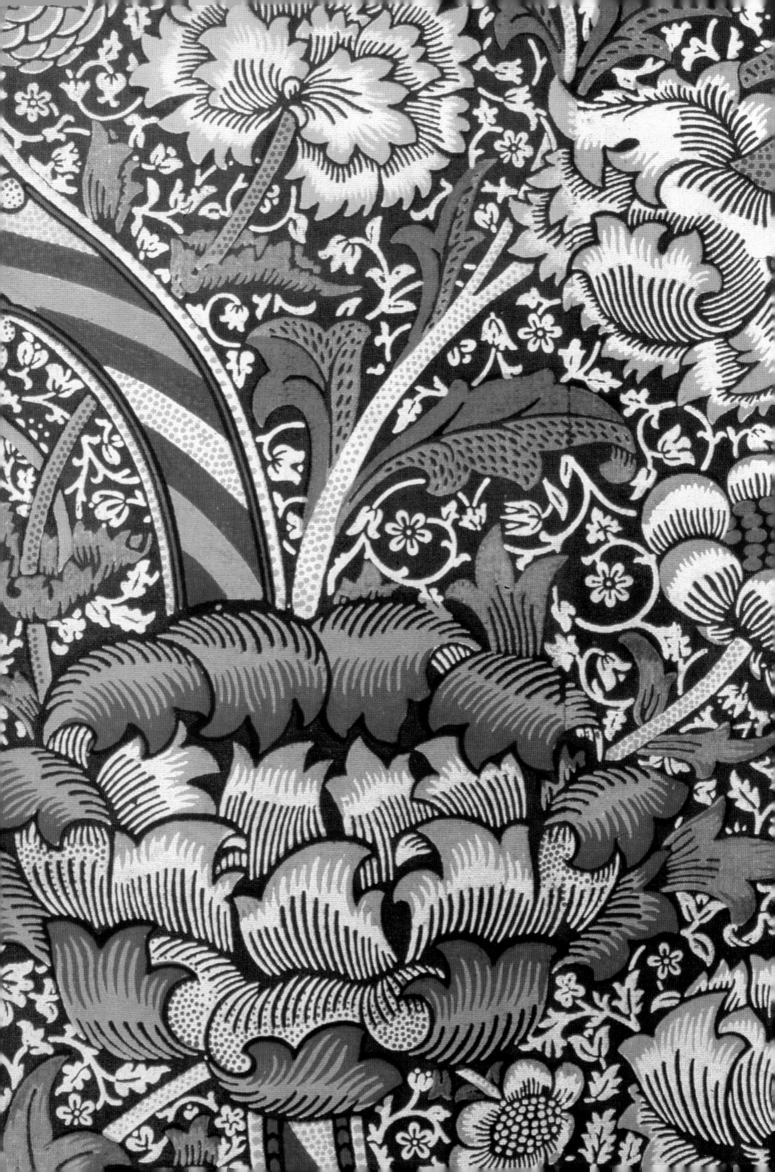

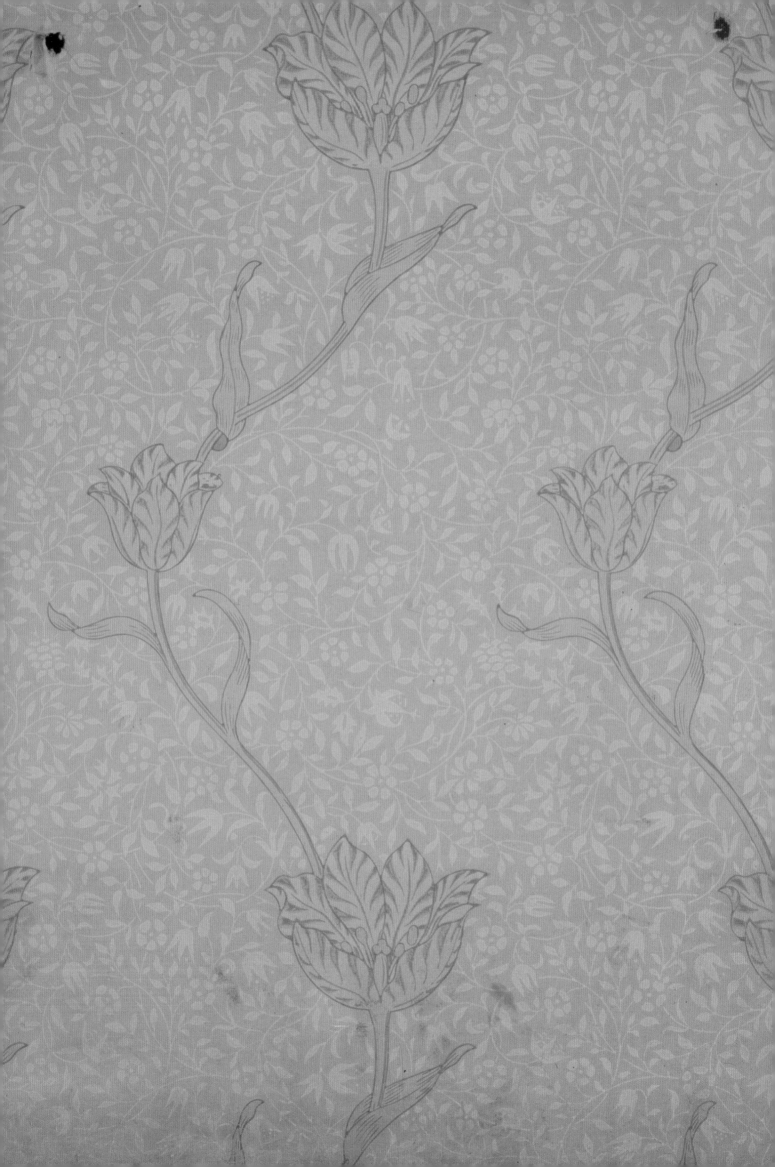

Artichoke Wallpaper

J. H. DEARLE, 1899; print design. Victoria & Albert Museum, London.
Morris & Co. continued to produce wallpapers long after Morris's death, well into the twentieth century. After Morris, J. H. Dearle became the firm's most prominent textile and wallpaper designer. He obviously worked hard to imitate the Morris style.

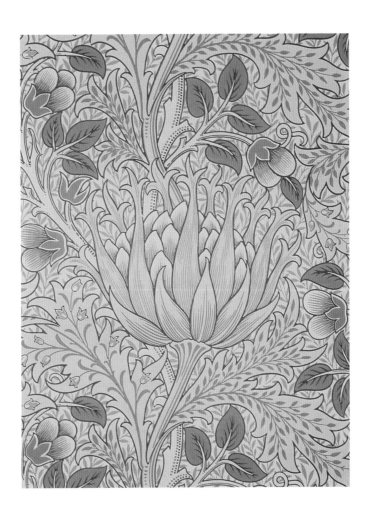

Garden Tulip Wallpaper

WILLIAM MORRIS, 1885; print design. Victoria & Albert Museum, London.
Strangely, Morris's peak years of political activity were also his most prolific years of wallpaper and textile design. Most Morris wallpapers are densely textured and complex. Occasionally, he opted for a starker, simpler design, as in *Garden Tulip*.

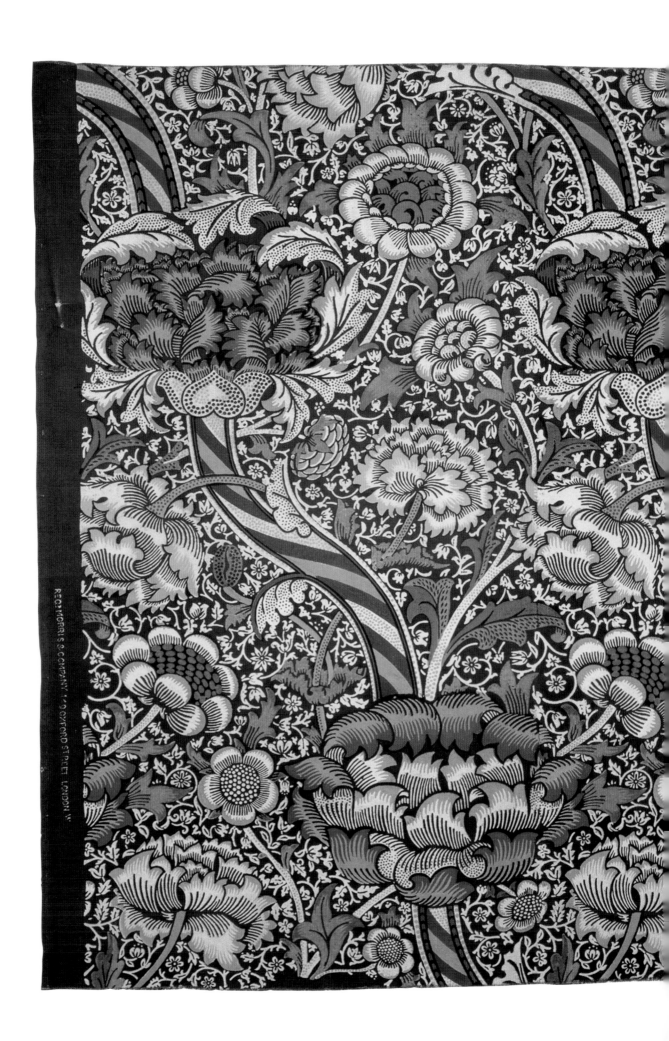

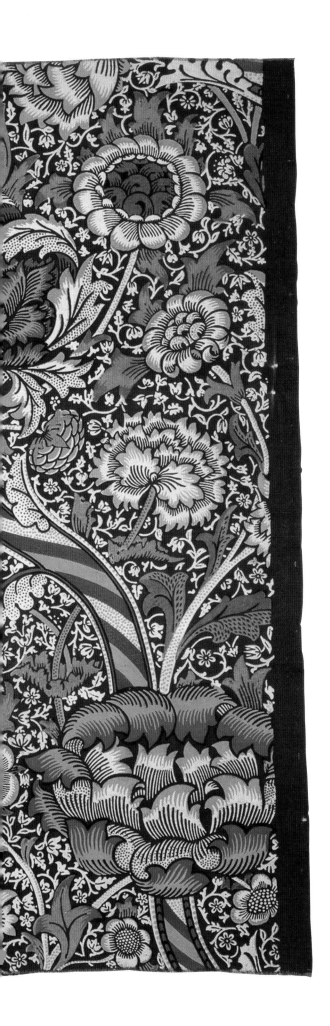

Wandle

WILLIAM MORRIS, c. 1880s; printed cotton.
Victoria & Albert Museum, London.
This chintz illustrates two recurrent
characteristics of Morris's printed cottons
from the 1880s. The diagonal motion
of the pattern is typical of his late work,
as is the use of the indigo dying technique
that Morris revived and popularized.

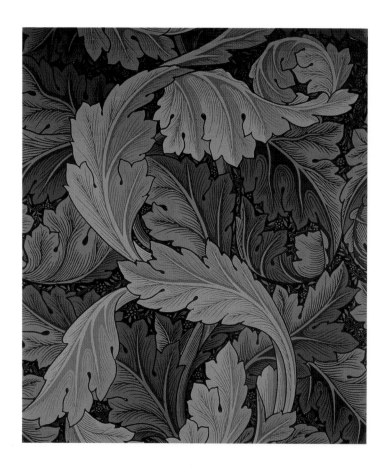

Acanthus Wallpaper

WILLIAM MORRIS, 1875; print design. Victoria & Albert Museum, London. Some of Morris's best wallpapers, such as *Acanthus,* create an illusion of depth on flat surfaces. To achieve a subtle variety of colors, thirty different blocks were used in the printing of *Acanthus.*

Snakeshead

WILLIAM MORRIS, 1876; printed cotton. Victoria & Albert Museum, London. Snakeshead, designed by Morris and printed by Wardle, is said to reflect Morris's familiarity with imported Indian textiles. He was also influenced by Italian, Oriental, and Persian designs.

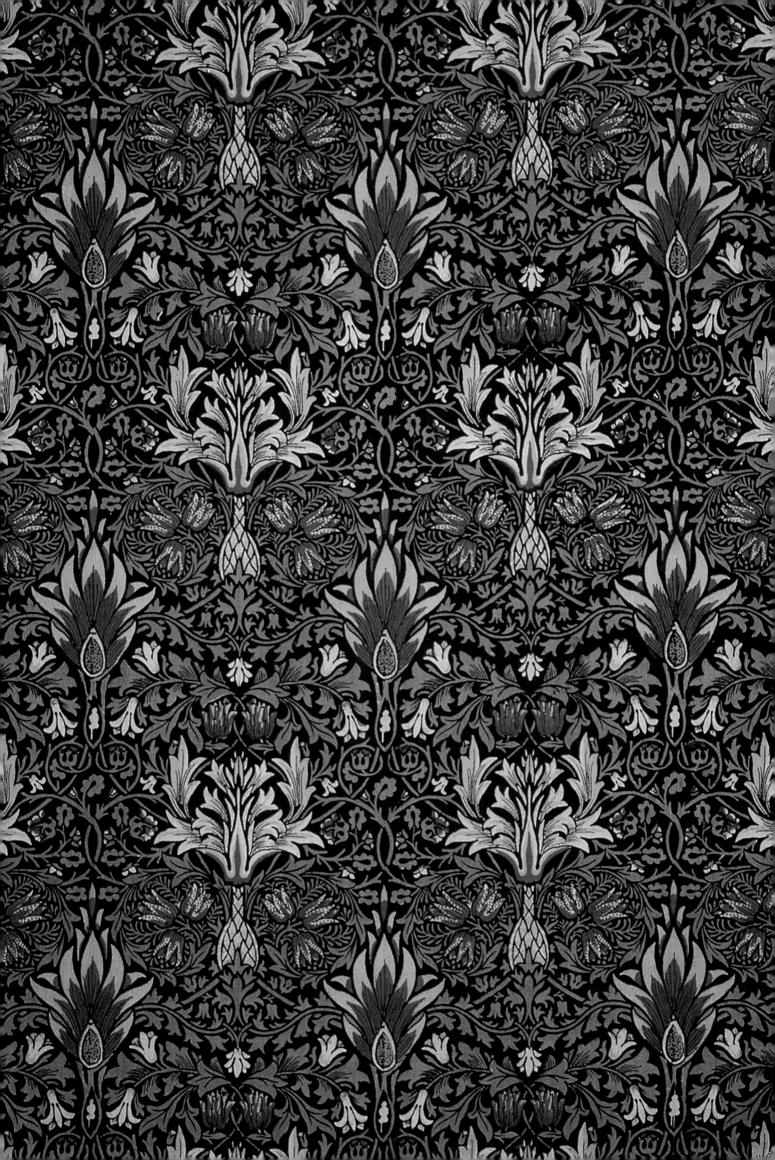

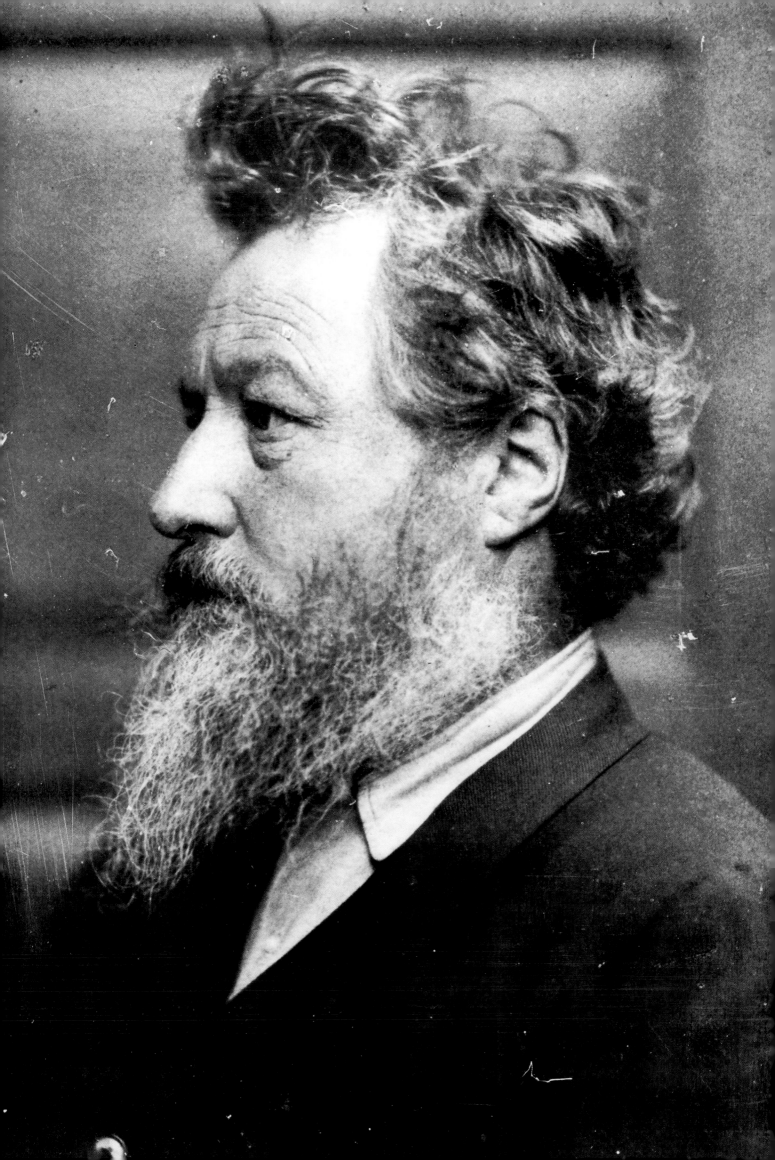

Chapter Four

IN SEARCH OF THE EARTHLY PARADISE

I do not want art for a few any more than education for a few, or freedom for a few .... rather than art should live this poor thin life among a few exceptional men, despising those beneath them for an ignorance for which they themselves are responsible, for a brutality that they will not struggle with,—rather than this, I would that the world should indeed sweep away all art for awhile ....

—from "The Lesser Arts"

When George Orwell wrote that, "The opinion that art should have nothing to do with politics is itself a political attitude," he inadvertently condensed William Morris's twenty-year struggle with the responsibilities of art into a single sentence.

To some, Morris's transformation from romantic to revolutionary appeared to be the sudden and drastic reversal of a wealthy man bitten by his conscience. In fact, Morris's understanding of the relationship between art and society had been there all along, obscured as it might have been by Rossetti's influence, the demands of running a business, and the ethereal detachment expected of serious artists. Although his work may have been the "embodiment of dreams," those dreams always had an important social dimension, be they poetic dreams of an old England untainted by industrialism or dreams of a band of modern artists uncorrupted by greed and expediency.

His entrance into the political realm demanded greater mental and physical toughness of him and, according to one of his doctors, may have shortened his life considerably, but Morris the socialist hardly stopped dreaming. He simply changed the orientation of his dreams and the medium through which he expressed them. He stopped looking backward for the ideal society and began looking forward. He significantly decreased his artistic output so that he might work instead on the minds and hearts of his fellow Englishmen. He associated less with the upper crust artistic elite and more with fellow socialists of all classes. And, so that none could accuse him of being an out-of-touch drawing room socialist, he hit the streets, proselytizing, lecturing at rallies, and distributing his numerous pamphlets.

The path of Morris's political development leads inevitably back to John Ruskin, the author who had first planted in his mind the notion that

William Morris

1890s, archival photograph.
The Hulton Getty Picture
Collection Limited.
Aged beyond his years from decades of strenuous activity and hard living, Morris retreated somewhat from the political world late in life and returned to his essential pleasures: writing and designing.

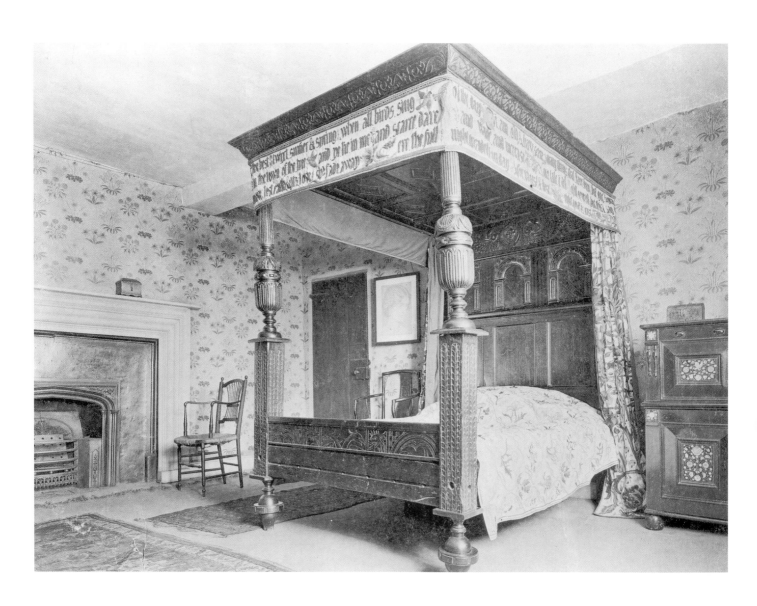

Morris's bedroom at Kelmscott Manor

c. 1871; archival photograph.

The Hulton Getty Picture Collection Limited.

The text above the bed reads: "The wind's on the wold/And the night is a-cold,/And Thames runs chill/Twixt mead and hill,/But kind and dear/Is the old house here,/And my heart is warm/Midst winter's harm." The walls are adorned with Morris's Daisy wallpaper.

Garden Tulip Wallpaper

WILLIAM MORRIS, 1885; print design.

Victoria & Albert Museum, London.

In *The Lesser Arts of Life*, William Morris wrote, "Whatever you have in your rooms, think first of the walls." He himself had been thinking of walls since he discovered that "room hung with faded greenery" in Queen Elizabeth I's hunting lodge in Epping Forest.

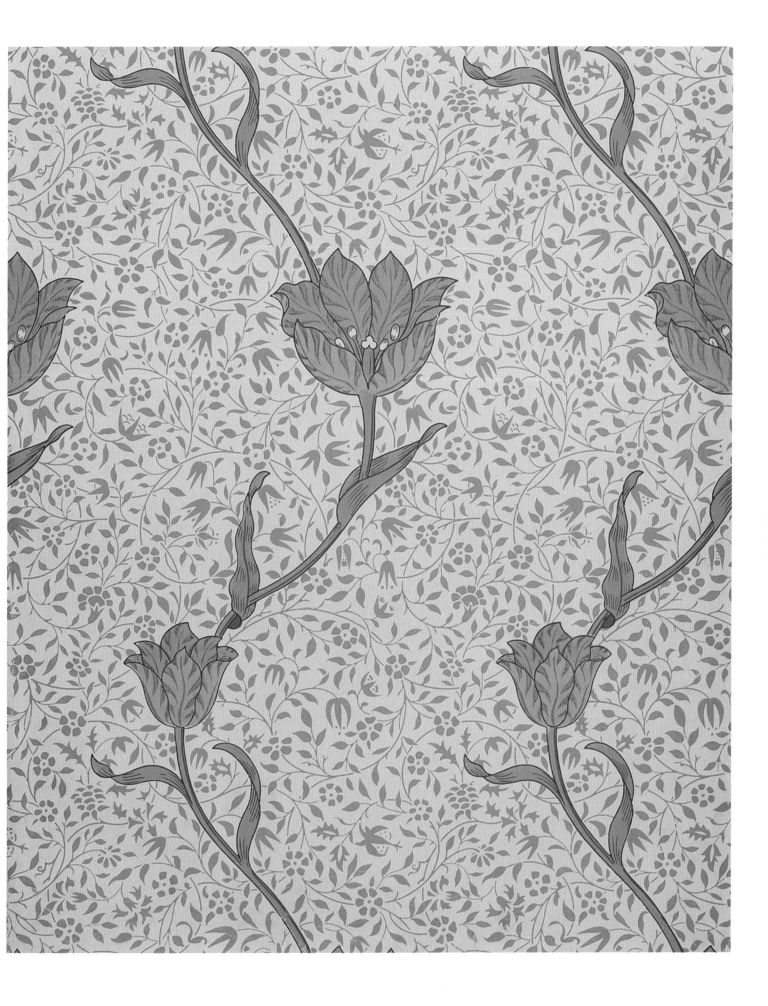

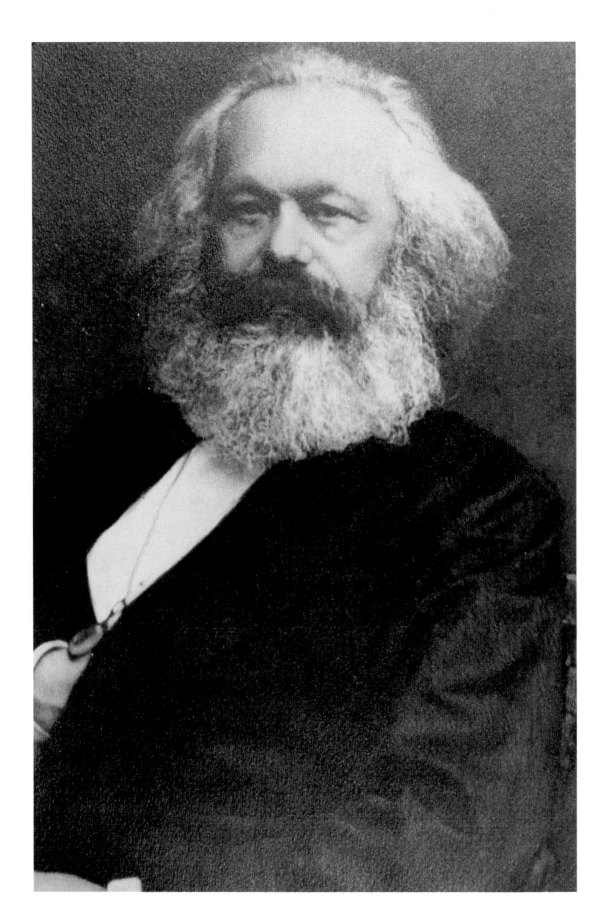

Karl Marx

Undated; tinted photograph.
The Bettmann Archive.
Morris claimed that
he had converted
to socialism before
reading Marx. He
did eventually read
Das Kapital and,
despite his self-
professed inability to
understand its eco-
nomics, regarded the
work as a landmark.

social change might be the prerequisite of artistic change. Ruskin used this perception to justify a highly conservative, autocratic political philosophy. That Morris should use the same insight to arrive at the opposite political stance is not surprising. In a similarly maverick fashion, Morris first learned his form of socialism not from Karl Marx but from the philosopher and economist John Stuart Mill's vehement critique of socialism. Both Ruskin and Morris agreed that the current social conditions were abhorrent. The solution lay in either a move back to medieval-like central authority or a move forward to true equality. Morris, at heart a sentimentalist who wanted badly to believe in the inherent goodness of human nature, chose the latter.

Despite the disapproval of his artist friends and the reluctant forbearance of his wife, Morris devoted himself to socialism with the same fervent passion he brought to art and poetry. The similarities do not end there. If the first two decades of his adult life had been spent attempting to beautify the world through decorative arts and poetry, the second two were characterized by a pursuit of the same goals through different avenues. However toughened by experience and disillusioned with the vicious cycle of commerce and profit, he remained at heart a Utopian dreamer, a passionate spokesman for possible futures.

A Poet of Renown: The Earthly Paradise and the Icelandic Sagas

By the early 1870s, William Morris was a very famous man. Although his firm was highly regarded, Morris earned his fame mostly through his poetry, especially his long poem *The Earthly Paradise*. The poem first appeared in 1868 and extended to four volumes over the next two years. Twenty years after its publication, when Morris's controversial reputation as a socialist writer and lecturer was firmly established, he would still frequently sign letters to the editors of newspapers and magazines, "William Morris, author of *The Earthly Paradise*." In its famous Prologue, *The Earthly Paradise* invites readers to

> Forget six counties overhung with smoke,
> Forget the snorting steam and piston
>   stroke,
> Forget the spreading of the hideous town;
> Think rather of the pack-horse on the
>   down,
> And dream of London small, and white,
>   and clean,
> The clear Thames bordered by its gardens
>   green.

The enormous critical and popular success of *The Earthly Paradise* suggests that the English audience, on the whole, accepted the invitation. A collection of twenty-four stories drawn

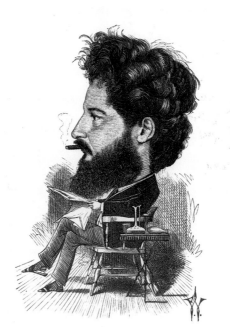

THE EARTHLY PARADISE.

Caricature of William Morris
Artist unknown, c. 1870s. Corbis-Bettmann.
The Earthly Paradise was Morris's best known and most beloved poetic work. Twentieth-century critics have been less kind to The Earthly Paradise, tending instead to favor his Icelandic sagas of the 1870s.

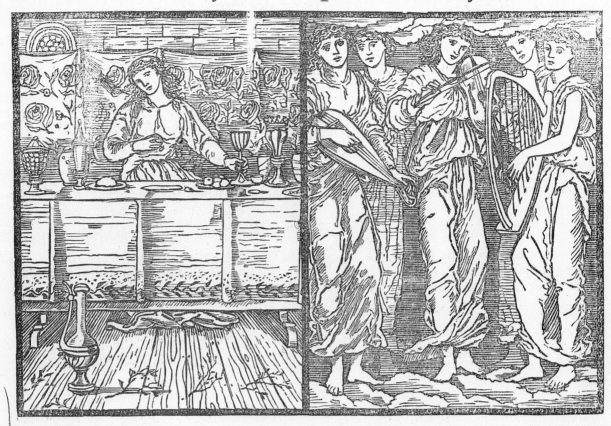

Argument.

Psyche was a King's daughter, whose beauty made all people forget Venus, wherefore the Goddess hated her, and would fain have destroyed her: nevertheless she became the bride of Love, but her sisters gave her such evil counsel that he was wrath with her, and left her: whereon, she, having first revenged herself of her sisters, wandered through the world seeking him, and so doing, fell into the hands of Venus, who tormented her, and set her fearful tasks to accomplish; but the Gods and all nature helped her, so that at last she was reunited to love, forgiven by Venus, and made immortal by the Father of Gods and Men.

Part I.

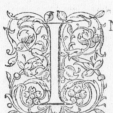

IN the Greek land of old there was a King
   Happy in battle, rich in every [thing,
But chiefly that he had a young daughter
   Who was so fair all men rejoiced [in her,
So fair that strangers, landed from the sea,
Beholding her, thought verily that she
Was Venus visible to mortal eyes,
Fresh come from Cyprus for a world's surprise.
She was so beautiful, that had she stood
On windy Ida by the oaken-wood,
And bared her body to that shepherd's gaze,
Troy might have stood till now with happy days,
And those three fairest all have gone away
And left her with the apple on that day.

And Psyche is her name in stories old
As even by our fathers we were told;
All this saw Venus from her golden throne,
And knew that she no longer was alone
For beauty, but, if even for a while
This damsel matched her God-enticing smile:
Wherefore she wrought in such a wise, that she,
If honoured as a Goddess, certainly,

Was dreaded as a Goddess none the less,
And pined away long time in loneliness.
   Two sisters had she, and men called them fair—
But as king's daughters might be anywhere,—
And these to lords of great name and estate
Were wedded, but at home must Psyche wait.
The sons of kings before her silver feet
Still bowed and sighed for her; in music sweet
The minstrels to all men still sung her praise,
While she must live a virgin all her days.
   So to Apollo's temple sent the King
To ask for aid and counsel in this thing,
And therewith sent he goodly gifts of price,
A silken veil wrought with a paradise,
Three golden bowls set round with many a gem,
Three silver cloaks, gold sewn in every hem,
And a fair ivory image of the God
That underfoot a golden serpent trod:
And when three lords with these were gone away
And must be gone now till the twentieth day,
Ill was the King at ease, and neither took
Joy in the chase, nor in the pictured book
The skilled Athenian limner had just wrought,
Or in the golden cloths from India brought.
At last the day came for those lords' return,

Psyche and her beauty.

Psyche hated of Venus,

Her sisters wedded, but she a virgin

The King sends to the oracle.

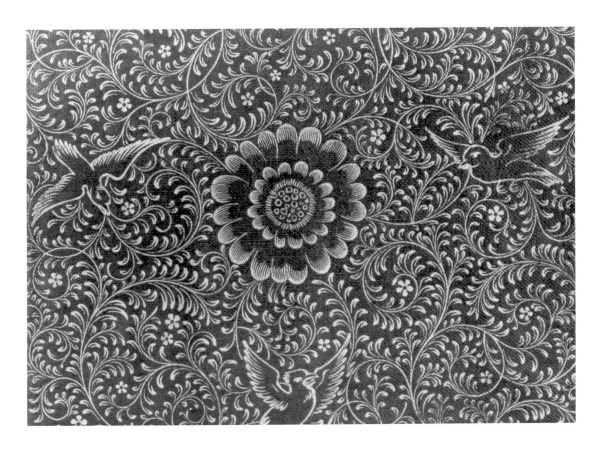

The Story of the Volsungs and Niblungs

detail of binding designed by William Morris and Philip Webb, 1870; William Morris Gallery, London. Despite the variety of media in which Morris dabbled, recurrent elements such as birds, flowers, and intertwining vines are characteristic of most of his work. This embossed book binding uses patterns similar to those found in Morris' many wallpapers and textiles.

from a wide variety of classical, medieval, and Norse myths and legends, *The Earthly Paradise* was viewed as family entertainment, content to tell rich stories in ambling, lyrical language, and generally unconcerned with symbolism and deeper meanings. It glorifies the past and offers it as an escape from the bustle of contemporary life.

In truth, the rendering of idyllic and simple worlds was an escape for Morris as well as for his readers, an escape not only from the age but from an increasingly turbulent personal and domestic life. In 1865, after a nearly fatal bout with rheumatic fever, Morris left the beloved Red House and moved his family to Queen Square in London so that he could avoid the long commute to work. Poor health would be a recurrent theme in the Morris family through-

out the next decade. Jane experienced frequent spells of a somewhat undefined sickness which occasioned many trips to spas and consultations with specialists. Morris's first daughter, Jenny, suffered from epilepsy. Under pressure from such domestic demands and a business perpetually on the verge of unraveling, Morris had taken to heavy drinking. George Warrington Taylor, the firm's business manager, pleaded with Morris at one point to reduce his wine consumption to two and a half bottles a day. It is unclear whether Morris followed Taylor's advice; what is certain is that he withdrew somewhat from the hectic affairs of the firm and entered into one of the most productive literary periods of his life.

Morris's knowledge of myth and legend was encyclopedic, as the phenomenal range of sto-

The Story of Cupid and Psyche

WILLIAM MORRIS, c. 1868; illumination. The Pierpont Morgan Library, New York. Written around the time of *The Earthly Paradise, The Story of Cupid and Psyche* features over seventy designs by Burne-Jones. Morris cut the wood blocks himself. *The Story of Cupid and Psyche* is one of Morris's first appropriations of classical mythology.

99

ries in *The Earthly Paradise* demonstrates. In the late 1860s, he developed an especially strong interest in Icelandic lore, an interest that would dominate his literary efforts throughout the 1870s. In 1868, Morris began studying the Icelandic language with a prominent scholar and translator, Eirikr Magnusson. The two published translations and adaptations of Icelandic sagas beginning with *The Saga of Gunnlaug Worm Tongue* in 1869. Magnusson was reportedly much like Morris in size and temperament, and the two enjoyed a productive and congenial partnership, developing an effective method of collaboration. Magnusson, far more adept at Icelandic grammar, would supply literal word by word translations which Morris then shaped into a lyrical English verse that was distinctly his. *The Story of Grettir the Strong* followed, and, next, the sweeping saga, *The Story of the Volsungs and*

the Niblungs. Morris was partially responsible for the translation and publication of three Icelandic sagas before, in 1871, he decided that a trip to Iceland was in order.

He regarded his two Icelandic sojourns as redemptive and rejuvenating escapes from a home life that had quietly become a suffocating hell. Rossetti had moved in with the Morrises at their Kelmscott Manor home and had probably already begun having an affair with Jane. Although he never explicitly acknowledged the betrayal, it is clear that Morris's attitude toward Rossetti, his former mentor, had changed drastically. In a letter to Coronio Aglaia, he wrote, "Rossetti has set himself down at Kelmscott as if he never meant to go away; and not only does that keep me from that harbour of refuge (because it really is a farce our meeting when we can help it) but also he has all sorts of ways so unsympathetic with the sweet simple old place, that I feel his presence there as a kind of slur on it." Later in the same letter, Morris writes, "O how I long to keep the world from narrowing on me, and to look at things bigly and kindly." Apparently, his trips to Iceland allowed him to do just that.

The rugged landscape and harsh climate enlivened him, as did the vigorous culture. Iceland freed him from the narrowing world and put him in touch with something deeper and purer than human entanglements. It added an edge to his poetry, a character, however, that Swinburne among others regarded as a coarse defilement of one of the age's sweetest and most refined poetic talents. Many Morris scholars go further, suggesting that the renewed zest he discovered in Iceland was a prime motivating force in the political career he was on the verge of launching. The cold of Iceland, its jagged landscapes and its stories, served as a wake-up call for the self-described "dreamer of dreams."

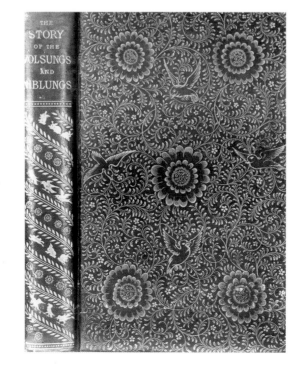

The Story of the Volsungs and Niblungs

Binding designed by William Morris and Philip Webb, 1870; William Morris Gallery, London. One of Morris's early collaborations with Eirikr Magnusson, *The Story of the Volsungs and Niblungs* was actually written before Morris had ever visited Iceland. Although his Icelandic sagas share common subject matter with Wagner's *Ring Cycle*, Morris was not at all fond of Wagner's work.

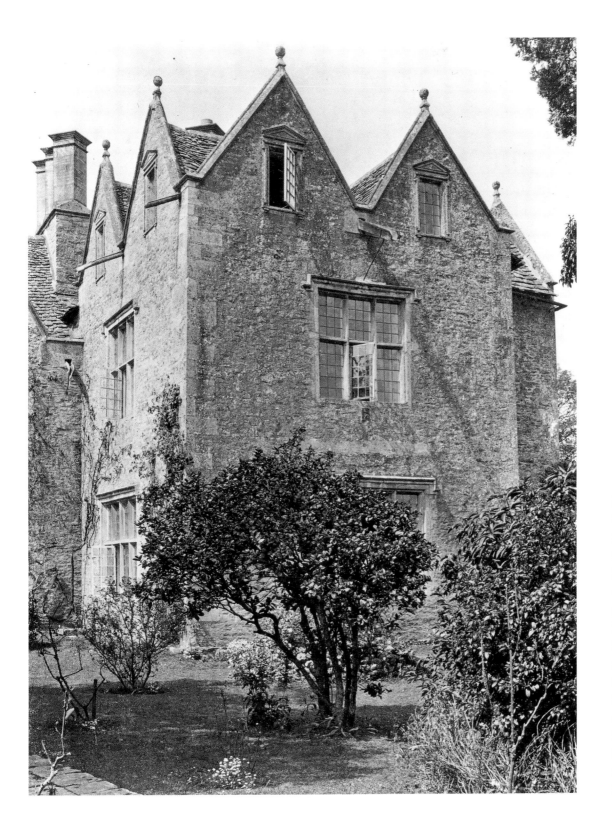

Kelmscott Manor, Oxfordshire

The Hulton Getty Picture Collection Limited.
Morris's favorite home was also the site of his greatest pain. Rossetti lived at Kelmscott with the Morrises and had an affair with Janey. During the early 1870s, Morris spent much of his time away from Kelmscott, either in Iceland or at his other residence, Kelmscott House, in London.

101

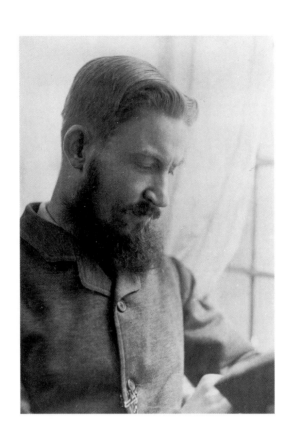

The Eastern Question and Anti-Scrape: Morris Enters the Fray

The revelations of Iceland had transformed William Morris into a more willful and active man. In the years immediately after his second trip there, Morris exerted his influence on several fronts. First, he took control of the firm in 1875, buying out the less productive partners and, in essence, banishing Rossetti from his, and Jane's, life. In 1876, he published his most acclaimed work of poetry, *Sigurd the Volsung*, another Icelandic saga akin to Wagner's *Ring Cycle* and later declared by George Bernard Shaw to be the greatest epic since Homer. These were also years of continued artistic growth—the mastery of dyeing and weaving and a return to manuscript illumination inspired by Georgiana Burne-Jones, the woman who had become his closest friend and

confidant in the difficult years of the early 1870s. Georgie, as he called her, had also quietly suffered the infidelity of a mate, and between them there was a deep, though exclusively platonic, understanding. His poetry of this period reflects a new willingness to directly acknowledge the darker side of his experience, especially his self-perceived failure at love, a theme that finds its fullest expression in *Love is Enough*, published in 1872.

All this new energy and candor fueled his interest and involvement in contemporary problems. Two events in particular politicized Morris. The crisis in Bulgaria, popularly known as the Eastern Question, angered scores of conscientious Victorian Englishmen, Morris among them. In 1876, the Turks violently suppressed an uprising of Bulgarian Christians, killing twelve thousand. British Prime Minister Benjamin Disraeli, far from intervening on behalf of the Bulgarians, threatened to declare war against Russia in defense of the Turks. Disraeli's political rival, William Gladstone, initiated organized dissent with the publication of *The Bulgarian Atrocities and the Question of the East*. Gladstone's return to the political scene coincided with Morris's arrival, and, at first, Morris considered himself a Gladstonian liberal. Later, Morris would find liberalism an ineffective and weakly conciliatory way of dealing with domestic problems. But in 1876, Morris was elected treasurer of the Eastern Question Association, and his political activity had officially begun.

When the Eastern Question Association disbanded in 1878, Morris thought that his short political career had come to an end. Such was hardly the case. In fact, he had already begun to pursue social change in an area to which he was more naturally suited. In the 1860s, the firm had participated in a general movement to restore medieval churches, a process that en-

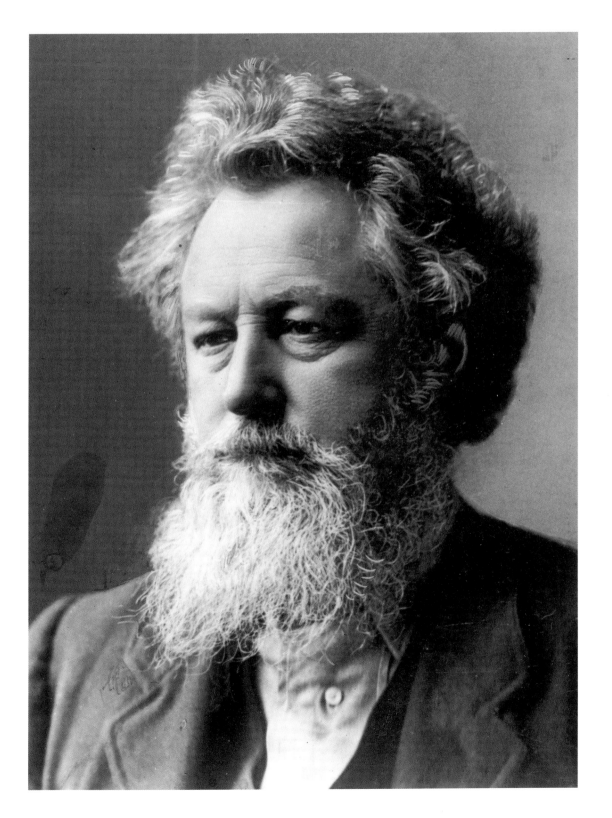

FOLLOWING PAGE:
Bookcase
detail; Morris, Marshall, Faulkner & Co., c. 1860s; Victoria & Albert Museum, London. "Have nothing in your houses which you do not know to be useful or believe to be beautiful." Morris's applied his credo with grace and practicality, creating home furnishings that were functional and attractive.

William Morris
1875; archival photograph. The Hulton Getty Picture Collection Limited. By the 1870s, William Morris was a famous poet and respected public figure. When he turned his attention to political issues, his reputation afforded him instant credibility. As he grew more radical, however, he incurred ridicule and frequent charges of hypocrisy.

103

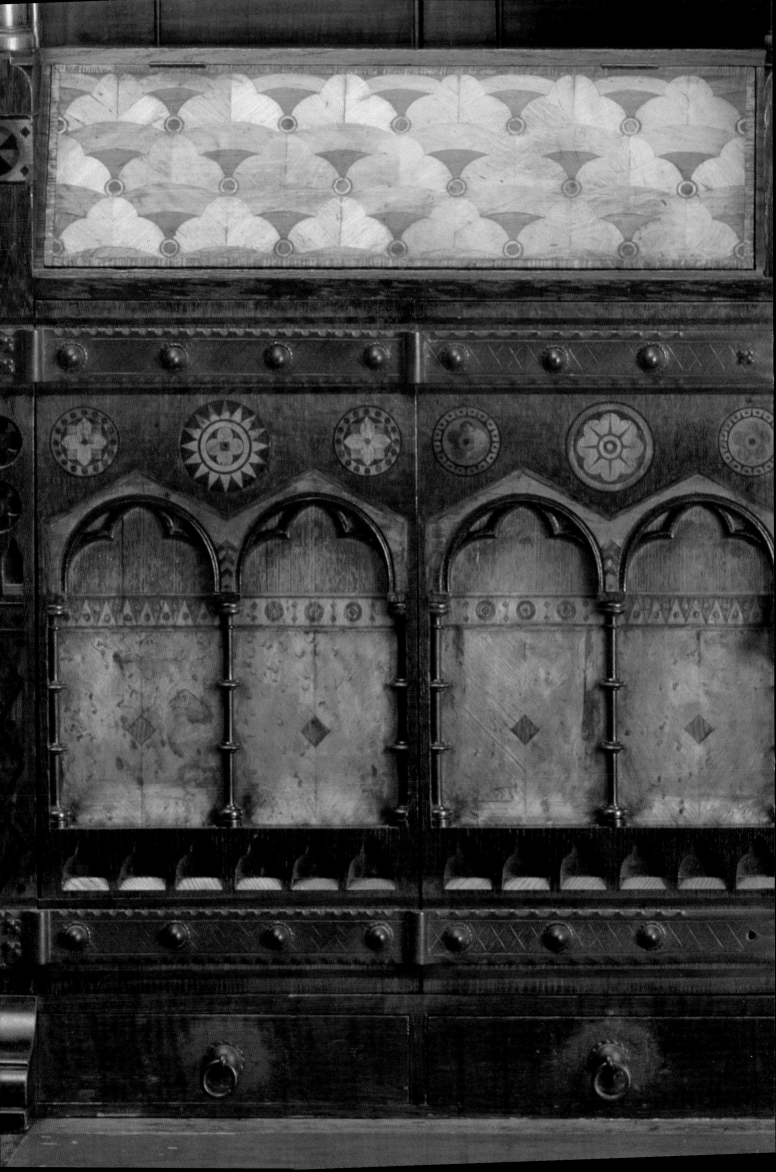

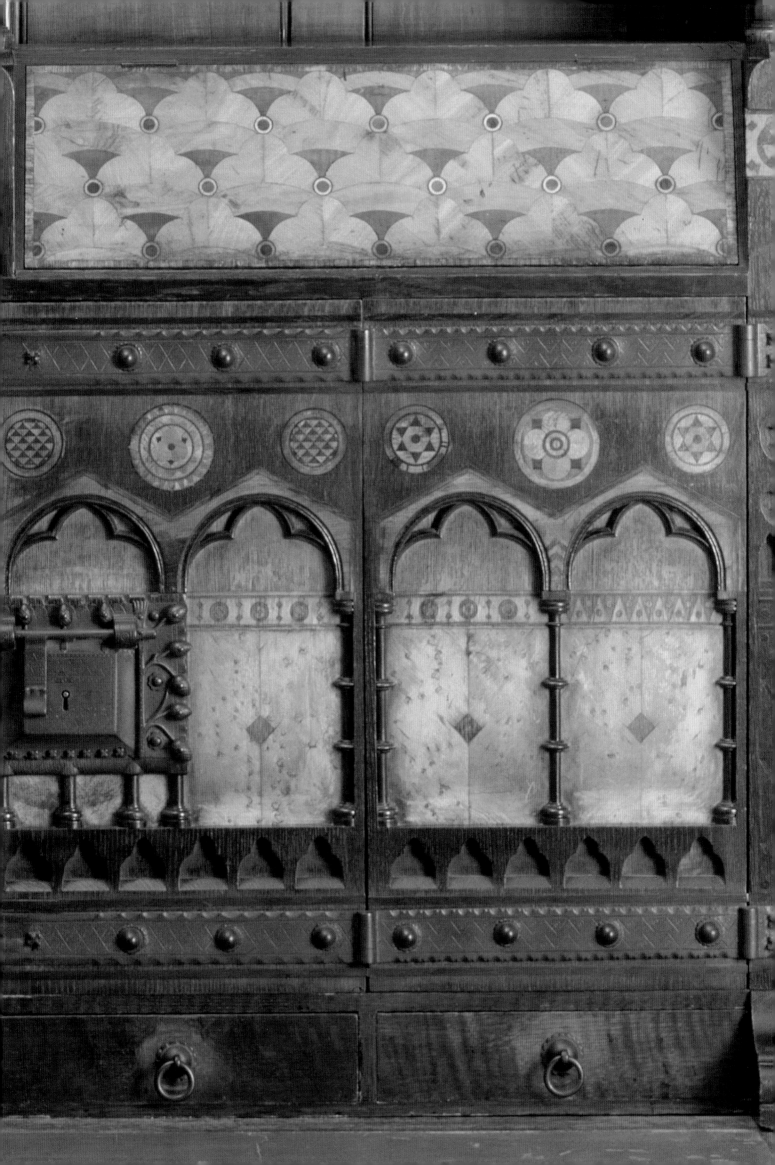

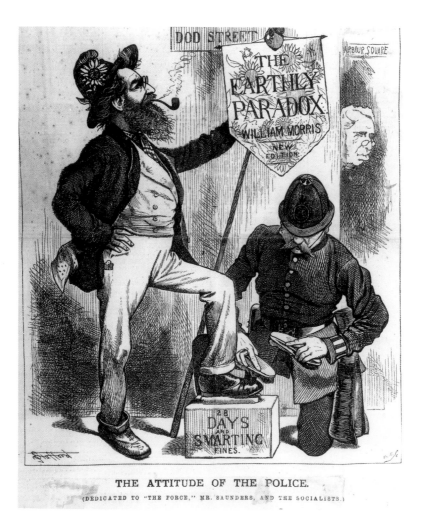

THE ATTITUDE OF THE POLICE.
(DEDICATED TO "THE FORCE," MR. SAUNDERS, AND THE SOCIALISTS.)

tailed the destruction of additions and modifications that had taken place after the original construction. Many of the firm's stained-glass designs were commissioned as a part of these restoration efforts. Morris's opinion on the matter had changed to such an extent that he became, in 1877, a founding member the Society for the Protection of Ancient Buildings, a group committed to resisting the restoration mania and preserving England's diversity of architecture. Anti-Scrape, as the movement came to be known, was instrumental in saving several churches in England and St. Mark's in Venice, Italy.

Anti-Scrape represented the fruition of Morris's lifelong interest in architecture. He would never design a building himself, but he would be responsible for saving several and raising awareness of the value of diversity and

the folly of historical uniformity. Perhaps G.E. Street, his mentor in Oxford, would not have been proud. Street, after all, had built his reputation on designing medieval revivals. Morris, however, had become a forward-thinker. As much as he had always been enamored of the styles and systems of medieval art and restoration, and had a reactionary longing for the old days in general, he realized that these beliefs no longer satisfied his desire for real change. Anti-Scrape could hardly be called a radical movement. Its interests and issues were primarily aesthetic, and most of the other prominent members, including Ruskin, Carlyle, and Burne-Jones, were politically conservative. Still, in this area of expertise and lifelong interest, Morris experienced his first success as an activist.

The Making of a Radical: The Social Democratic Federation and the Socialist League

As William Morris moved steadily to the political left, he incurred the contempt and venom of those who had been his friends, his clients, and the literary establishment that had adored his poetry but abhorred his politics. Even among the socialist ranks, his revolutionary ideology and his refusal to advocate change through established political systems made him an anomaly, a wealthy businessman who, upon conversion to socialism, out-radicalized the radicals. When Morris gave himself over to socialism, he did so completely, abandoning all faith in liberalism and conventional channels and investing himself entirely in a socialist future attainable only through revolution. Even so, he continued to run his business, to keep servants in his two houses, and to visit the Burne-Jones's home for dinner every Sunday. He thus left himself vulnerable to accusations of duality and hypocrisy from both socialists and opponents of socialism. Apparent contradiction, of course, had never stopped Morris in the past and would not stop him now.

In 1882, Morris joined the Democratic Federation, a socialist organization founded a year earlier by Henry Mayers Hyndman, with whom Morris would co-author *A Summary of the Principles of Socialism*. Reactions within the organization were mixed. Hyndman himself was glad to have a prominent figure aboard and welcomed the attention Morris would bring. Other members doubted the depth of his commitment to the cause. They knew Morris as a poet and the maker of fine and prohibitively expensive furniture, a dubious track record at best for an aspiring socialist. Eager to demonstrate his earnestness, he dedicated himself to the legwork of socialism. He distributed literature, both his own pamphlets and the Federation's

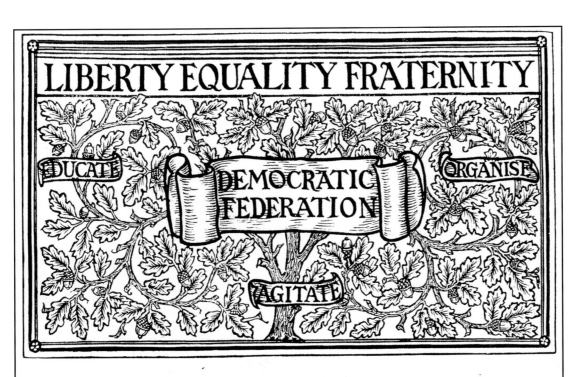

Membership card for the Democratic Federation

WILLIAM MORRIS, c. 1880s; woodcut design. The Hulton Getty Picture Collection Limited. Morris did not abandon art entirely when he converted to socialism. This card, designed for H. M. Hyndman's Federation, bears some of the trademark floral characteristics of Morris's textile designs.

LIBERTY EQUALITY FRATERNITY

EDUCATE DEMOCRATIC FEDERATION ORGANISE

AGITATE

MEMBERSHIP CARD FOR DEMOCRATIC FEDERATION
DESIGNED BY WILLIAM MORRIS
FROM THE ORIGINAL BLOCKS

H. M. Hyndman

1919; archival photograph. UPI/Corbis-Bettmann.
Hyndman and Morris disagreed on the function of a socialist organization. Hyndman favored a more conventional political party while Morris wanted little to do with Parliament. It was Hyndman's Federation, however, that launched Morris to political prominence.

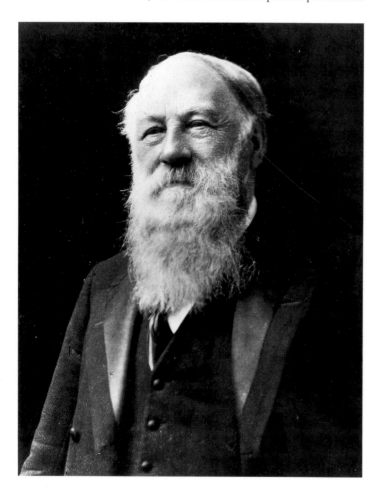

weekly paper, *Justice*. He lectured, attended rallies, and, in one instance, got himself arrested in the act of resisting the police at a riot. Respect was hard to win; when, after his arrest, he was let off almost apologetically by a magistrate who knew his literary reputation, Morris was satirized in political cartoons as the beneficiary of double standards.

In time, Morris grew dissatisfied with Hyndman and the Federation. At the root of his displeasure was an ideological schism within the group. Hyndman, whom Morris had begun to view as a political careerist, wanted to turn the Federation into a conventional political party that put up candidates for Parliament and worked for specific reforms such as higher wages for workers. Morris, much in favor of equality and better working conditions, objected vehemently to this notion. In his view, the purpose of a socialist organization was simple: to make more socialists, to advance the spread of socialist thought and sentiment, and to prepare for the inevitable, and inevitably bloody, revolution. Morris had also wearied of the inefficiency of Federation meetings. He had little patience for factious squabbling, a particularly socialist tendency that Morris parodied in the beginning of his socialist Utopian romance, *News From Nowhere*: ". . . there were six persons present, and consequently six sections of the party were represented . . . ." At meetings, he was often less than gracious, pulling hairs from his mustache and uttering "damn fool" repeatedly in response to other speakers.

Disagreements within the fold forced Morris to clarify his own position. In 1884, he split from Hyndman's Federation, and taking a small section of the group with him, formed the Socialist League. With "Education towards Revolution" as its motto, the Socialist League catapulted Morris to prominence as a political figure. The journal *Commonwealth* was begun in 1885 with Morris as its editor and financier. A profusion of pamphlets followed, some of them among his best known and most respected writings and lectures: *Useful Work versus Useless Toil, How We Live and How We Might Live, Art and Socialism*, and *How I Became a Socialist* among many others. Many admirers of Morris's poetry found his socialist essays coarse and slightly mad. Others, however, believe that in these pamphlets Morris seriously challenged his own intellect for the first time. His verse, "the embodiment of dreams," had come easily to him. Political clarity did not. In his essays, he critiqued current social conditions with a sharp and persuasive wit, conjured up compelling images of a socialist future, and, of course, prophesied the revival of art under new conditions of brotherhood and equality.

Predictably, Morris's passionate political involvement took a toll on his social and personal life. Jane Morris, accustomed to house visitors of a different, more refined sort, shrunk away from the new type of guest William was bringing home. Although the Burne-Joneses remained faithful friends, they attributed Morris's loss of humor to his overboard socialism. Of all his friends and colleagues, only Philip Webb, Charles Faulkner, and daughter May Morris followed him into socialism. Even more depressing to Morris was the failure of the Socialist League, or rather its hijacking by a small band of anarchists within. Morris left the league in 1890 and founded the Hammersmith Socialist Society. But by then his faith in imminent revolution had waned. The Hammersmith Society, a small and cultured group, busied itself with lectures and publications, just as often about art as about revolution. Morris, by now a grand old patriarch of British socialism, hosted weekly meetings at Kelmscott Manor. He continued to believe in the cause. In fact, he had learned to give his uncommonly extreme form of socialism another name: communism, "a change which would destroy the distinctions of classes and nationalities."

Morris had little strength or energy left to pursue this change. For all his effort, he had never established communication with the working classes. His political views were largely unappreciated in his own time, both by his more conservative artist friends and by other socialists, including Marx's partner Friedrich Engels, who had great hopes for Morris but later dismissed him as "politically untalented" and too sentimental. Morris would have agreed wholeheartedly. And because of his aversion to political solutions, his uncompromising insistence on a real change in the basis of society, not mere temporary modifications, Morris proved ultimately to be prophetic. His reputation as a political thinker has grown considerably in the twentieth-century.

Friedrich Engels
1877; archival photograph.
Corbis-Bettmann.
A leading socialist and Marx's collaborator, Engels celebrated Morris's conversion to socialism at first. Later, after reading Morris's pamphlets, Engels dismissed Morris's brand of socialism as too sentimental and idealistic.

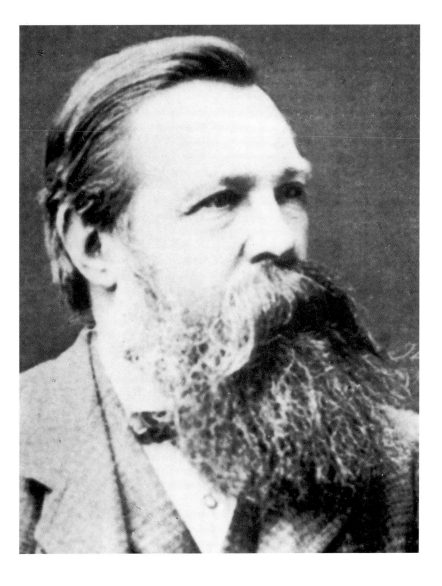

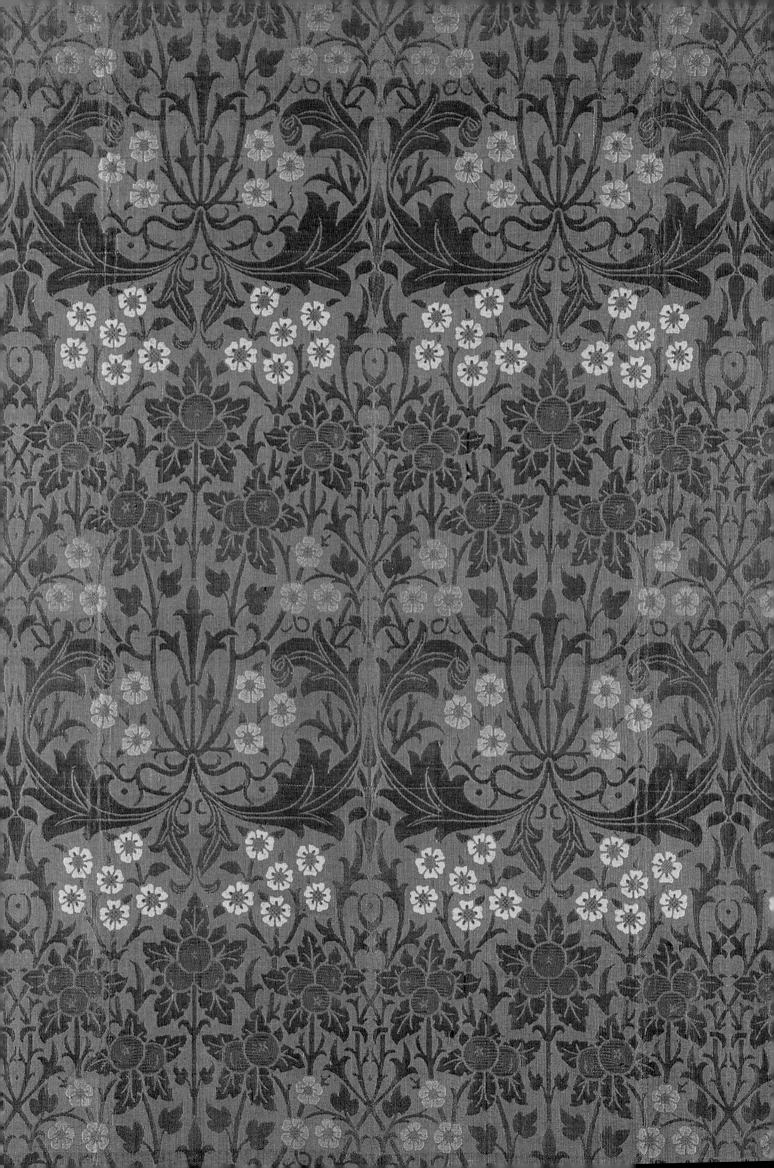

The Life of Ten Men: Kelmscott Press and the Death of William Morris

Exhausted from his efforts in the political realm and recurrently ill throughout his last six years, William Morris still mustered the energy to tackle one new creative enterprise: book printing and publishing. Once again, his efforts would prove to be innovative and influential. The Kelmscott Press, operated out of the Kelmscott Manor home he had maintained since the early 1870s, began in 1891 by publishing Morris's most recent prose and verse romances: *The Glittering Plain, Poems by the Way, The Well at the World's End*, and, in 1893, *News From Nowhere*. Morris then turned to his own back catalogue, publishing new editions of *The Defence of Guenevere, The Life and Death of Jason*, and the first volume of *The Earthly Paradise*. As if summing up his career, he also used the Kelmscott Press to print volumes of some of his favorite authors, including works by

Ruskin, Rossetti, and a highly regarded edition of Chaucer.

In his final years, Morris is credited with the development of two type faces, "Golden" and "Troy." The Kelmscott books were fine objects of art, printed on handmade paper and bound in pigskin. Some were illuminated, others graced with engravings and borders by Burne-Jones. In all, Kelmscott Press produced a remarkable fifty-three titles in less than eight years. His printing techniques and preferences were influential well into the twentieth-century, yet another of Morris's lasting contributions to art. Morris expert Ray Watkinson has referred to the Kelmscott Press as "a cornerstone of modern typography."

Apple

J. H. DEARLE, 1895–1900; woven linen and silk; Victoria & Albert Museum, London.

Between 1895 and 1900, J. H. Dearle experimented with silk and linen mixtures and produced a series of famous woven textiles named after fruits. Dearle, who assumed more responsibility at the firm in Morris's late years, lacked Morris's expertise with small background patterns, but was otherwise considered his equal as a designer.

THIS IS THE PICTURE OF THE OLD HOUSE BY THE THAMES TO WHICH THE PEOPLE OF THIS STORY WENT. HEREAFTER FOLLOWS THE BOOK IT-SELF WHICH IS CALLED NEWS FROM NOWHERE OR AN EPOCH OF REST & IS WRITTEN BY WILLIAM MORRIS.

Frontispiece from News from Nowhere

WILLIAM MORRIS, 1893; woodcut design. Corbis-Bettmann.

News from Nowhere combined Morris's talent for rendering idyllic worlds with his socialist agenda. It describes the dream voyage of a Victorian Englishman to an idealized socialist future. It concludes, ". . . if others can see it as I have seen it, then it may be called a vision rather than a dream."

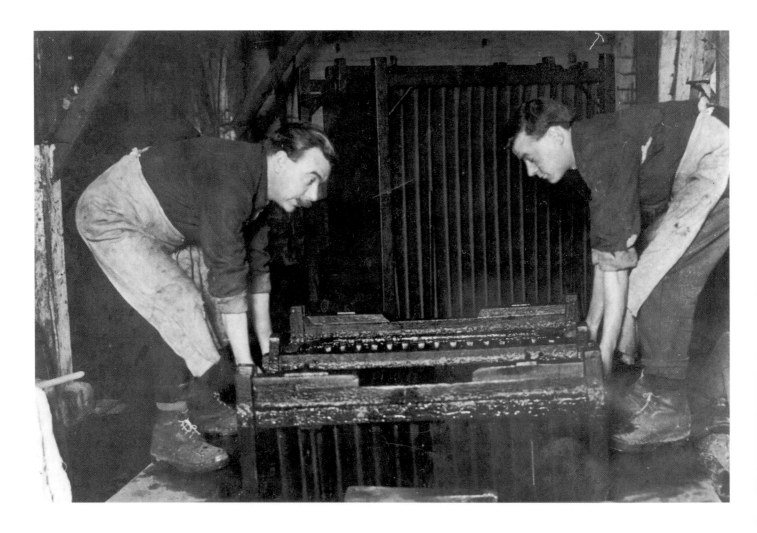

Merton Abbey Works

1930s; archival photograph. William Morris Gallery, London. Workers dye cloth at the firm's Merton Abbey workshop. Morris & Co. continued to produce popular wallpapers and cotton prints well into the twentieth century.

Morris continued to work on Anti-Scrape, design tapestries and wallpapers, and write books as well. His two final literary works, published posthumously, were *The Water of the Wondrous Isle* and *The Sundering Flood*, both prose romances of the kind he had been imagining and writing since he was a young man. Described by George Bernard Shaw as "a startling relapse into literary Pre-Raphaelitism," his final works seem to indicate a retreat into his imagination, a place far removed from the political turmoil that had commanded his attention for years. Yet Morris continued to attend and lecture at socialist meetings. When aroused by a particularly sensitive issue, such as tree-cutting in Epping Forest, he would once

again bring the force of his public personality and his fiery rhetoric to bear.

He knew no other way to live but to create, to write, and to rail against all that offended his refined but broad and inclusive sensibilities. After he designed his final wallpaper, "Compton," Morris turned those duties over to his daughter May and to J.H. Dearle, the new manager at the firm's Merton Abbey works. Early in 1896, Morris delivered his last of countless public lectures, "One Socialist Party." In July, he left Kelmscott for the last time, attempting a return to the northern countries that had so fired his spirit and imagination. The trip was a dismal failure. Morris was too frail to leave the ship. In September, he

🍃 Frederico tertio Romanorum imperatore regnante, magnum quoddam ac pene divinum beneficium collatum est universo terrarum orbi a Joanne Gutenbergk Argentinensi novo scribendi genere reperto. Is enim primus artem impressoriam in urbe Argentina invenit. Inde Maguncíam veniens eandem fœliciter com⁄plevit.

I wold demaunde a question yf I should not displease, How many Knyghtes ben ther now in Englond that have thuse and thexercyse of a Knyghte? That is to wete, that he knoweth his hors & his hors hym, that is to saye, he beynge redy at a poynt to have al thing that longeth to a Knyght; an hors that is according and broken after his hand, his armures and harnoys mete and fytting and so forth, et cetera.

🍃 There is no good man blamed herin, hyt is spoken generally, late every man take his own part as it belongeth and behoveth. And he that fyndeth hym gylty in ony dele or part therof, late hym bettre and amende hym, and he that is veryly good, I pray God kepe hym therin.

Specimens of William Morris's Types

WILLIAM MORRIS, c. 1890s. Corbis-Bettmann. The Kelmscott Press books featured border and margin designs by Morris (over 600 in the Kelmscott *Chaucer*) as well as original print types. Pictured here are the *Golden*, *Chaucer*, and *Troy* types.

reluctantly terminated plans to produce a Kelmscott Press edition of Malory's *Morte d'Arthur*, the work that had been a holy text to the brotherhood and the narrative source of so many of Morris's own romances.

Late in September, Morris suffered severe congestion in his lungs. After finishing off the last lines of *The Sundering Flood*, he retired to his bed for the last time. His life's work, remarkable for its vigor, diversity, influence, and sheer abundance, was complete. Edward Burne-Jones

and Philip Webb attended him daily. On October 3, 1896, William Morris died at the age of sixty-two and was buried in Kelmscott churchyard. One family doctor echoed the popular sentiment that he had been done in by the disease of socialism. Many had felt that Morris's politics were a strange and unhealthy distortion of his essentially artistic nature. But those who knew him well understood that his socialist work had enriched him as much as it had drained him, that his political involvement had been a logical and compassionate extension of his art. Another more sympathetic doctor memorably diagnosed the cause of death and offered a kind of no-nonsense eulogy that Morris would have appreciated: Morris had died from "simply being William Morris and having done more work than most ten men."

Homage to Morris in Elysium
WALTER CRANE, c. 1890s; drawing. William Morris Gallery, London. Crane pictures Morris after his death in Elysium, the paradise of the blessed in classical mythology.

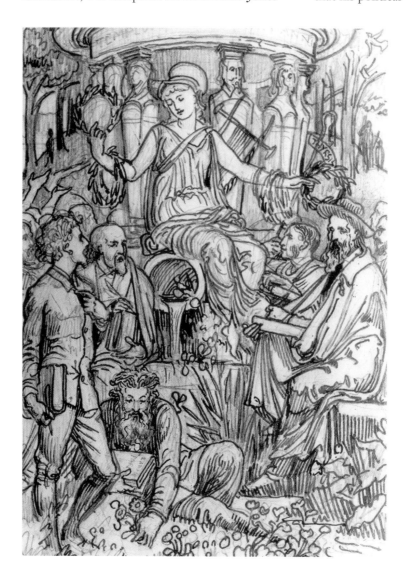

Bower
WILLIAM MORRIS; print design; Victoria & Albert Museum, London. In the 1880s, the peak of Morris's political career, he discovered a new zest for floral designs and produced the majority of his most famous wallpapers and chintzes during this period. Designing must have been an escape from the public world, a return to his childhood in Epping Forest.

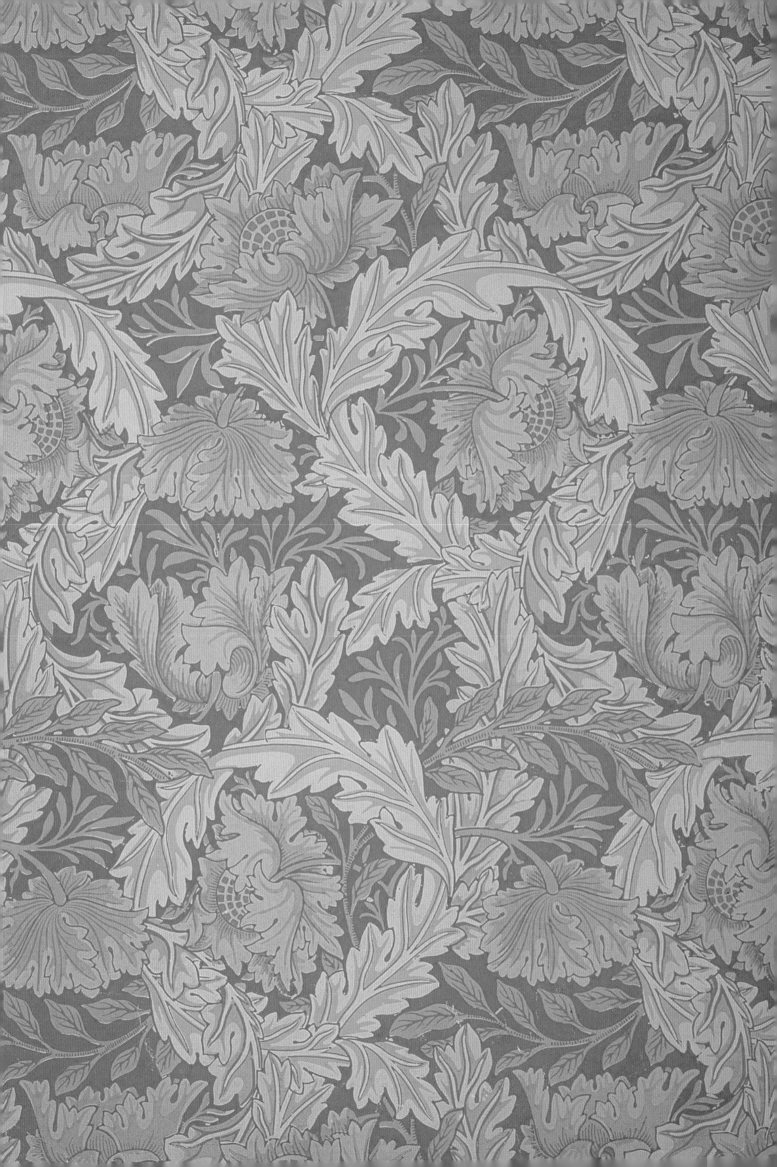

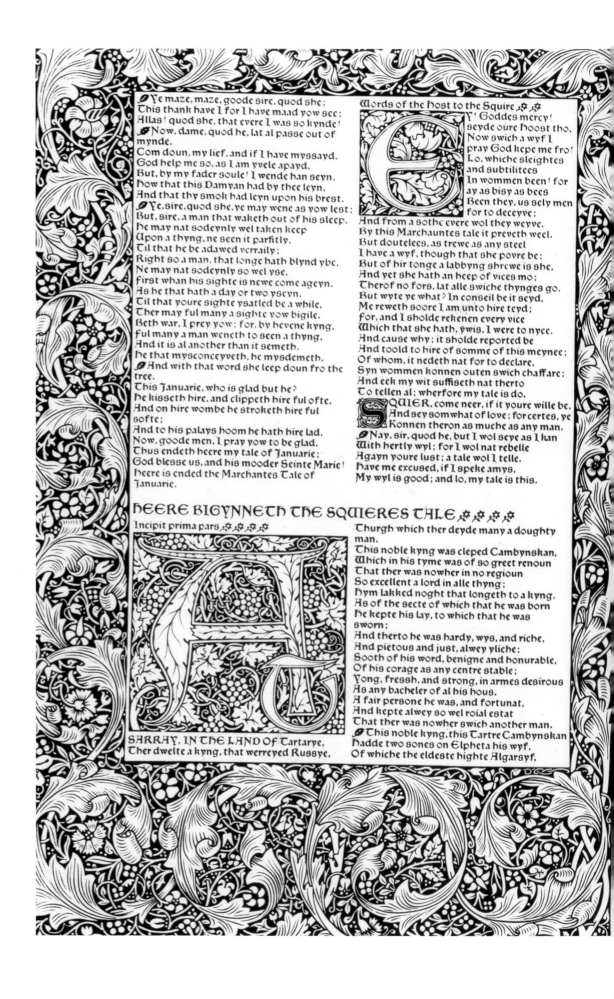

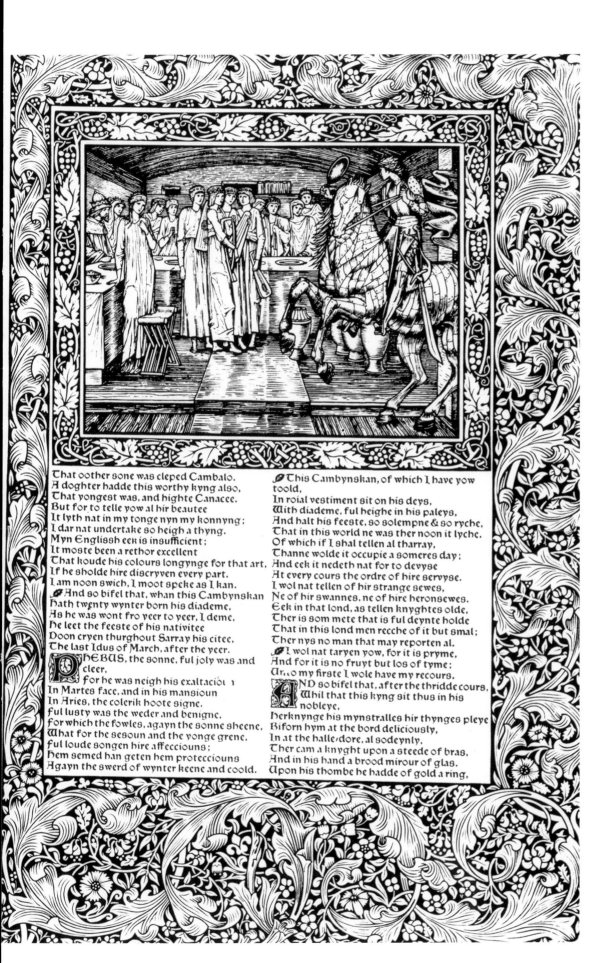

The Kelmscott Chaucer

WILLIAM MORRIS, 1890s; illumination; The Hulton Getty Picture Collection Limited. The Kelmscott Chaucer is perhaps the most famous production of the Kelmscott Press. It is certainly the most involved and ornate. Most Kelmscott books, however, were not as intricately bordered and designed. Morris reserved such grand treatment for his favorite of all English poets.

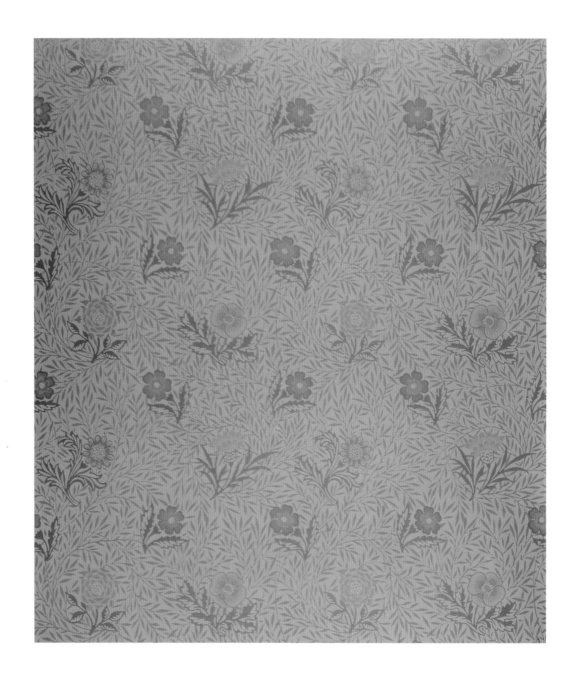

Powdered Wallpaper

WILLIAM MORRIS, 1874; print design.
Victoria & Albert Museum, London.
The *Powdered* design was later adapted
as a chintz. The background, sans
flowers, was also reproduced in 1895 as
the *Little Scroll* or *Willow* printed fabric.

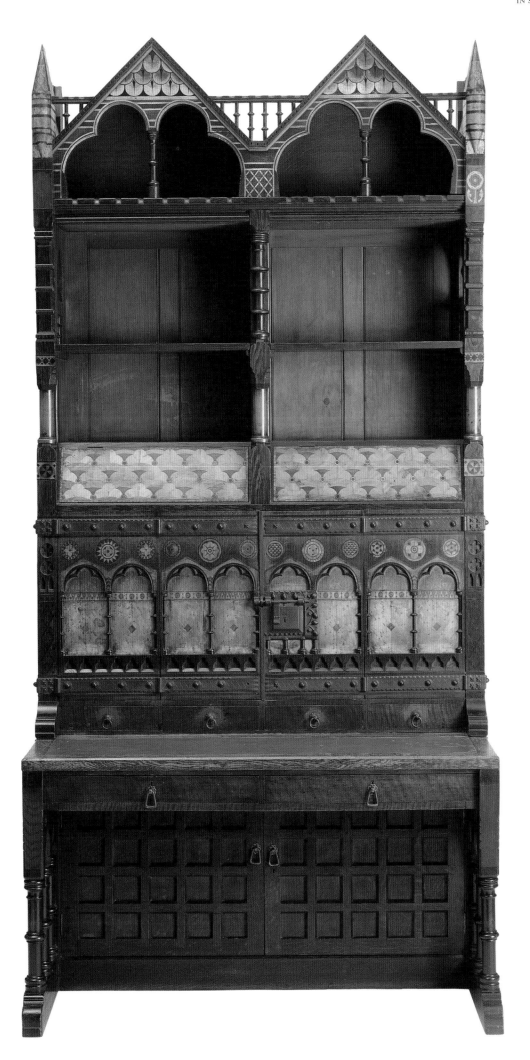

Floral Tiles

Morris & Co., n.d.; painted ceramic tiles. Victoria & Albert Museum, London. Elaborate floral designs remain the signature of the Morris style. Although the firm stopped producing ceramic tiles in 1880, Morris's intricate florals continued to dominate his work until the end of his life.

Bookcase

Morris, Marshall, Faulkner & Co., c. 1860s. Victoria & Albert Museum, London. Large and expensive items such as this oak inlaid bookcase were all the rage in suburban London. It was said that no home was complete without something from Morris & Co.. Ironically, Morris's popularity among the wealthy classes fired his interest in a socialist revolution.

119

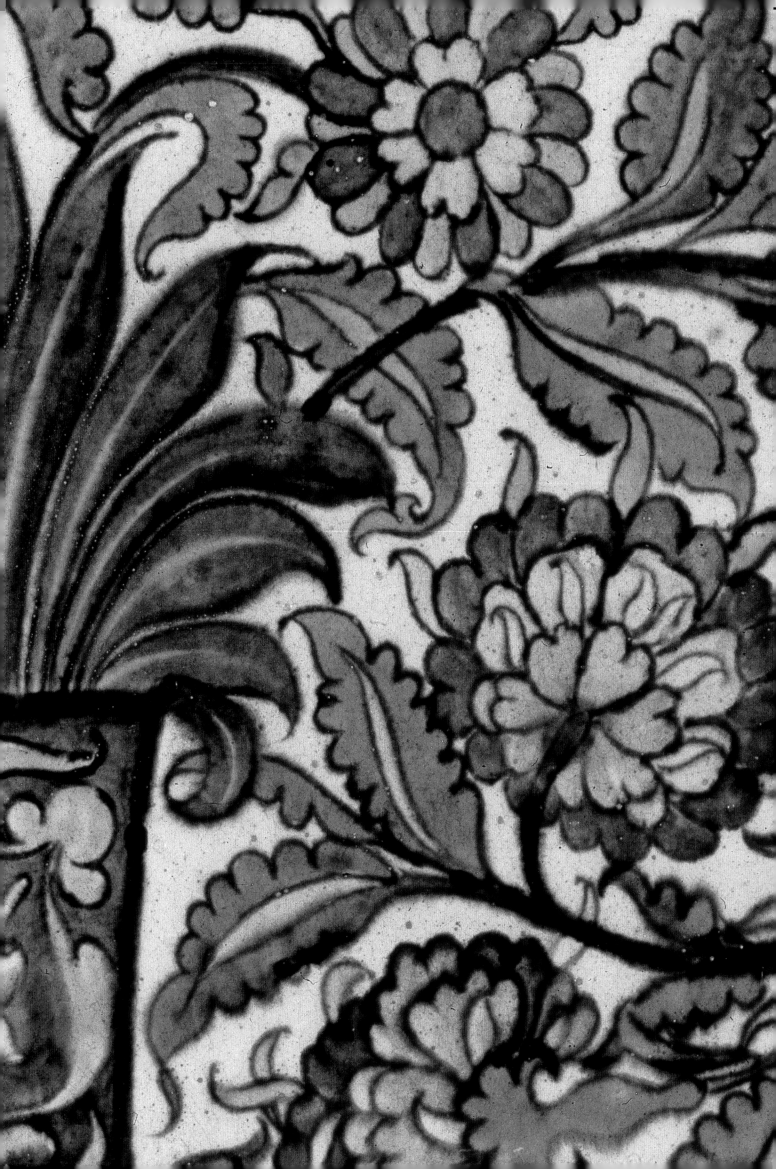

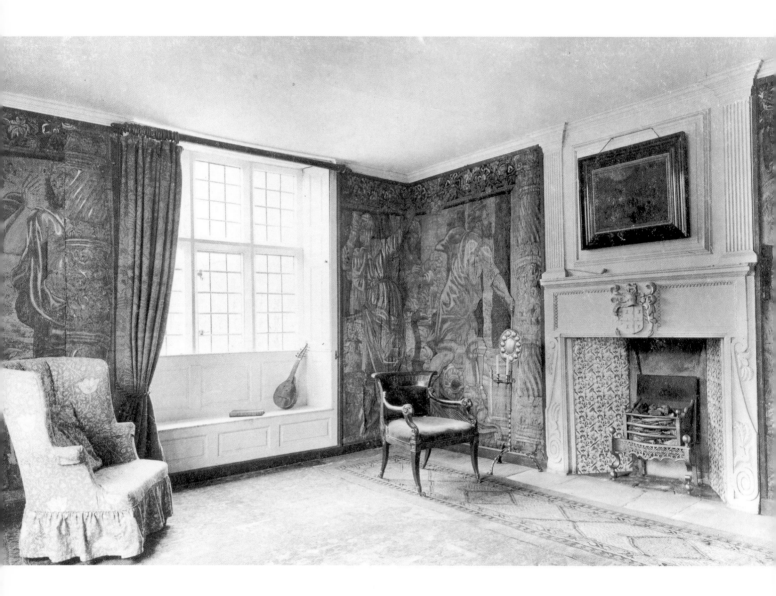

Interior of Kelmscott Manor

c.1871; archival photograph. The Hulton Getty Picture Collection Limited.
Of all his residences, Morris loved Kelmscott Manor best,
even though his work in London required that he keep
a residence there as well. Morris rented Kelmscott Manor
from the 1870s until his death. Janey Morris finally
bought the manor in 1913, one year before her death.

**Kelmscott Press Mark
from News From Nowhere**

*WILLIAM MORRIS, 1893; interlocking decorative
writing with signet. Corbis-Bettmann.*
A Kelmscott Press mark similar to this
one appeared in all of the Kelmscott
volumes. Book printing was Morris's
final artistic endeavor. Next to a good
house, Morris considered a good book
to be the highest kind of functional art.

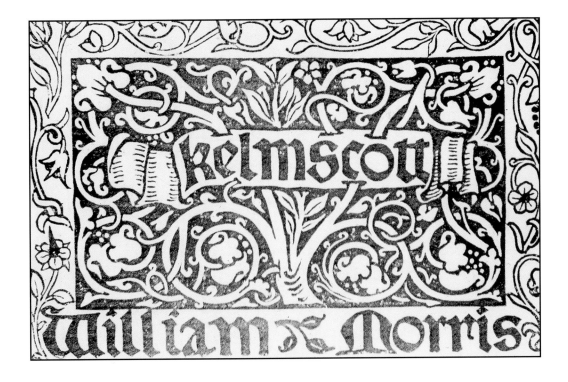

Tile panel design

WILLIAM DE MORGAN, 1876; ceramic tile. Victoria & Albert Museum, London. Many of the firm's tiles and ceramics, including this one, were designed by the famous potter William de Morgan. Morris & Co. stopped producing tiles in 1880.

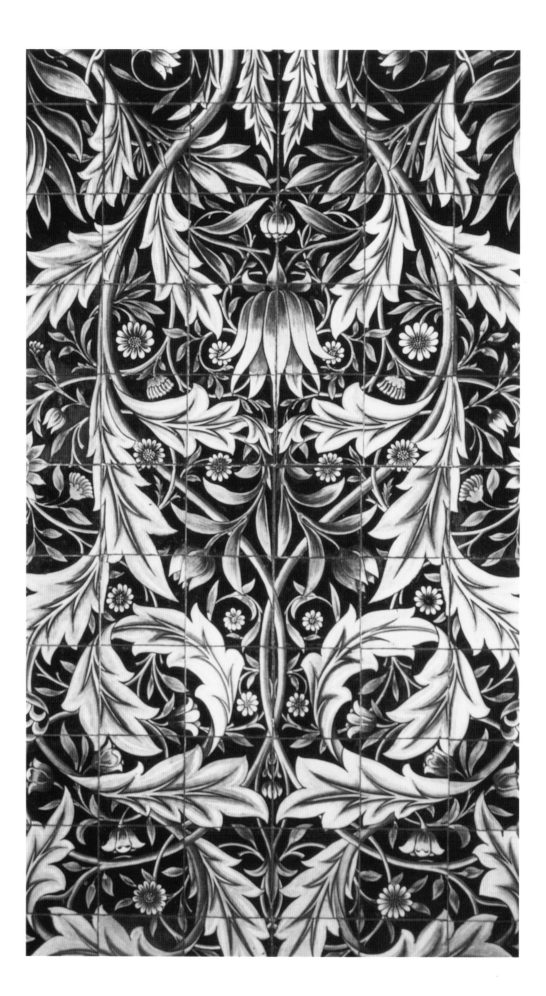

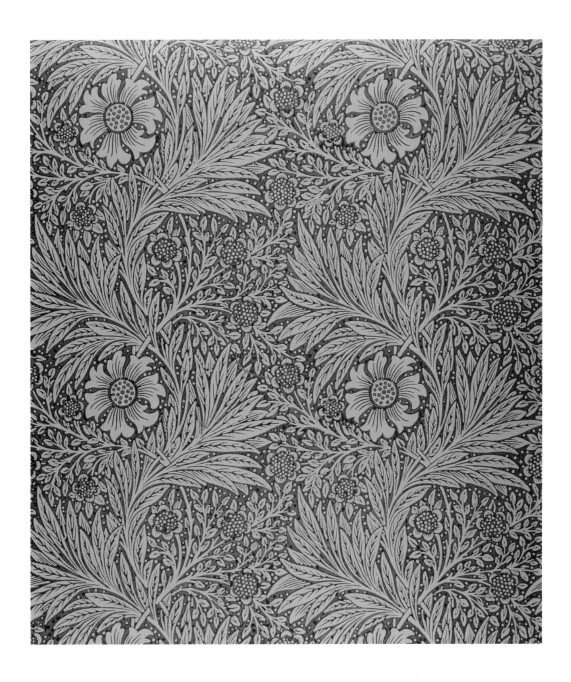

Marigold

WILLIAM MORRIS, 1875; print design; Victoria & Albert Museum, London.
Morris preferred wall hangings—chintzes and tapestries—to wallpaper, but the consuming public apparently did not agree. Many of
his printed fabrics, including *Marigold*, also sold well as wallpapers.

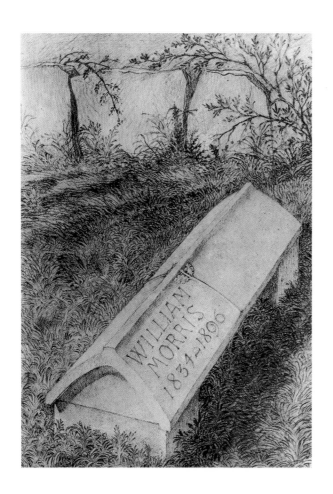

William Morris's tomb, Kelmscott Churchyard

Artist unknown; drawing.
William Morris Gallery, London.
Morris probably would have approved of the unassuming simplicity of his tombstone. His last weeks were spent awaiting death in the company of his best friends, Edward Burne-Jones and Philip Webb.

"Love Fulfilled" from A Book of Verse

WILLIAM MORRIS, 1870. Victoria & Albert Museum, London.
In the early 1870s, Morris devoted much time to illuminating manuscripts and producing borders and engravings for his poetic works. Much of the work of this period was dedicated to or at least inspired by Georgiana Burne-Jones, with whom Morris had an extremely close relationship.

LOVE FULFILLED.

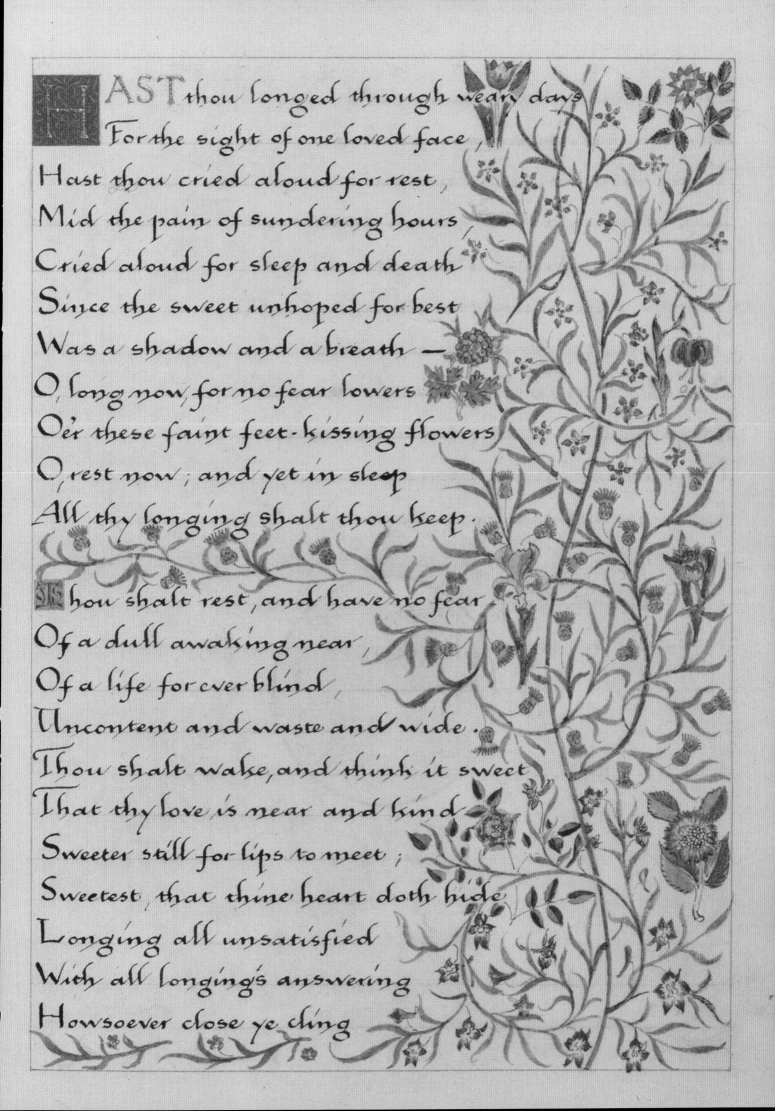

HAST thou longed through weary days
For the sight of one loved face,
Hast thou cried aloud for rest,
Mid the pain of sundering hours,
Cried aloud for sleep and death
Since the sweet unhoped for best
Was a shadow and a breath —
O, long now, for no fear lowers
O'er these faint feet-kissing flowers
O, rest now; and yet in sleep
All thy longing shalt thou keep.

Thou shalt rest, and have no fear
Of a dull awaking near,
Of a life for ever blind,
Uncontent and waste and wide.
Thou shalt wake, and think it sweet
That thy love is near and kind
Sweeter still for lips to meet;
Sweetest, that thine heart doth hide
Longing all unsatisfied
With all longing's answering
Howsoever close ye cling

INDEX